Jasmine Baucham

THE VISION FORUM, INC.
SAN ANTONIO, TEXAS

For my family—you become more and more precious to me with each passing day.

Table of Contents

Introduction

Five years ago, if I could have somehow foreseen that moment in history—April 7, 2010 (which also happens to be my twentieth birthday)—I would have been ecstatic. Ever since I was a little girl, I have loved to write. My first "novel"—penned at the tender age of eight—was a study in melodrama, a World War II story that centered around the gruesome events of the holocaust, in which every single character, including the narrator, died. Subsequent novels were soon to follow, from ten to fifteen, when I penned what I thought at the time was my *magnum opus,* a 70,000-word offering (roughly the length of the book you hold in your hands), again about World War II, and this time, a love story.

Five years ago, if you had told me that I would be publishing a book at the age of twenty, I would have been bursting at the seams . . . until you said it was nonfiction. And then I—who am on record having said that I would never submit a book for publication unless it was Pulitzer Prize worthy—would have balked. What on earth could I have to offer of the nonfiction persuasion—I who had collected prize-winning novels over the years so that I could read them and see what it took to be great—I who had read and reread my favorite literary works over and over again, to the point where they were falling apart at the binding—I who spent every spare moment working on novel after novel, building dreams of literary fame . . .

I would have asked you what sort of advice a twenty-year-old would have to offer her peers about life. I would have asked you why I wasn't in college getting that English/History double major or screenwriting degree I was vacillating between.

I'd ask, "What on earth am I writing about anyway?"

If you had answered, "Stay at home daughterhood," well . . . perhaps I would have fallen into a dead faint.

Perhaps I would have glanced venomously at the beautiful hardback that Mama had brought back from a homeschool conference on my fifteenth year, the one that disgusted me to such a degree that I shoved it back onto the shelf. Maybe I would have refused to read it then, even after my mother told me that I wasn't allowed to read another book until I had given it a fair chance. Maybe I would have stretched out the six weeks I defiantly put off obeying my mother. Instead of cutting my two books a week down to no books for six weeks, I might have held out even longer.

Maybe my mom would have forgotten her ultimatum, and perhaps life would have gone on as it had been. A junior in high school, I would have continued on the fast track to the college of my choice, despite the fact that my parents had voiced their strong reservations about me going so far away to school, and warned me about the dangers of a secular university. Maybe I would have ignored all of the warning signs that were telling me to reevaluate my choices, from the exposé I read about the dangers of the particular university I was considering to my parents' frank discussions with me on the subject of homemaking: "Sweetheart, you just don't seem interested in learning how to manage a home at all—in fact, you seem to *despise* the home. What's gotten into you?"

Even if I had never read the book, I still would have started to notice my mother in a way I never had before. To see her putting her family before herself on a daily basis—to watch her homsechooling my brother and me after seven years of teaching in the public school system, having graduated *cum laude* from one of the nation's biggest historically black colleges—to see this intelligent, beautiful, God-honoring woman walking Proverbs 31:10-31 in living color. I marveled at her.

"How did you sacrifice so much to be at home with your family?" I must have asked her one hundred times as I neared sixteen.

Mama smiled the same sort of smile you notice on the Mona Lisa—there was a peace and a stillness inside of her that I could not comprehend. "There's no place I'd rather be."

For me, homemaking was something that a woman did if she did not have the talent to do anything else. I was not that woman. In fact, I had decided, as per 1 Corinthians 7, that my spiritual gift was singleness, and that raising children in the nurture and admonition of the Lord and becoming a helper suitable to a godly man was not really something that I wanted to do. I was bottled-up lightening ready to be set loose on the world at large—I was going to be renowned. The only catch to my master plan was that I just kept seeing my mother, day in and day out, not using her words as much as her actions to show me the beauty of a homeward calling.

And I did read that book. *So Much More* by Anna Sofia and Elizabeth Botkin. You could say that it ruined my life—at least the dreams that I had built for myself. It brought the contradictions that I'd blindly accepted into sharp focus, and it showed me that I had accepted the culture's idea of success, and had come to let mainstream society define me where God's Word should have been doing the defining.

If you had told me at sixteen that I was going to be writing a book about stay-at-home daughters in four years, I would have laughed at you. There was already a book out there about stay-at-home daughterhood. I had read it, and it had changed my life. It had showed me principles that I had never considered before, such as:

How Genesis 2 relates the account of the creation of Eve, Adam's suitable helper, and, by extension, tells all women something important about their nature as helpers and completers.

How passages like Numbers 30 and Deuteronomy 22 point to the fact that, normatively, a daughter was her father's responsibility until he gave her in marriage.

How it has only been in the past one hundred years, since the advent and spreading of the feminist movement that women—both married and unmarried—have forsaken the sphere of home, and have borne Adam's curse (Genesis 3:17) and the brunt of a lack of protection.

How I had, without question, believed the notion that a married woman is worthy of nurturing, protection, guidance, and discipleship, and has been given a clearly defined role in her home (Titus 2:3-5), while single women were left on their own.

From the book for which I continue to be grateful, I learned the foundations of a truth that should have been obvious to me from the beginning. The reason the message is not obvious—the reason the message is countercultural—the reason the message is offensive—is because we have been so inundated with feminist ideology that it has become second-nature for us to reason through its lens. I had been told that I was smart, I was capable, and that I was a visionary. It never occurred to me that those gifts could be used to further my family's vision, to further the kingdom of Christ in the very sphere where he'd placed me: my home.

A few short months after I started this massive paradigm shift, just weeks after I had come to the decision not to go off to college after I graduated that year, I was blessed to be part of the documentary that followed *So Much More—Return of the Daughters*. In so many ways, the documentary answered the number one question on a Christian parents' mind when confronted with the idea of a daughter living at home until marriage under the tutelage of both of her parents with a view towards multigenerational faithfulness and discipleship: What does that look like?

At the time, I was seventeen, relatively new to the stay-at-home daughter concept, but so excited about all that I hoped the Lord would accomplish through my obedience to his calling on my life. I was my father's full-time research assistant, as well as the coordinator for his online bookstore. Several months after the movie was shot, I began to blog about some of the lessons I was learning as a result of living in my father's house. At first, I was blogging to a number of friends—and then, I began blogging to friends of friends—pretty soon, I was blogging to a host of strangers. Some were like-minded sisters in Christ, faraway friends and co-laborers.

Still others (the first of whom cropped up during the 2008 election season, the first year I was able to vote and the year I was the most vocal about politics as I have ever been on my blog or will probably ever be again) were far from friends and co-laborers. Some were fellow Christians who disagreed vehemently with my views. Most were unbelievers who read *Joyfully at Home* like one watches a spectator sport.

For the most part, though, the direct feedback that I received was positive. I had no idea how many daughters there were like me, who needed encouragement as they forged ahead in their countercultural decision. They were not getting ripped to shreds by gossip forums or receiving nasty anonymous comments on their blogs, but they were out in the real world answering real questions from real people. They were in there homes, day by day, striving to walk upright before the Lord as they served in that sphere. They were going to church every Sunday and ministering to other young women there. They were reaching out to their community in beautiful and diverse ways.

It was then that I started to despise the term that so well defines what we do: stay-at-home daughter. I hated it because it had become so very monolithic, when, in reality, what we girls are doing is so incredibly diverse.

If you would have told me at nineteen that I would be writing a book at twenty, I would have told you that I hoped I was up for the task. I would have said that I hope I can encourage young daughters striving to serve at home with my words; that I hope I would be able to convey the beauty and diversity of a homeward calling through my book, to right some misconceptions and help other daughters to do the same, and to help instill confidence and inspire industry in a generation of daughters who are daring to break from the mold of popular culture.

At twenty, I have been a "stay-at-home-daughter" for three years now, since I graduated high school in 2007. What I write here is the result of some of the lessons I have learned by living at home, some of the struggles and triumphs with which I am sure many other daughters in my situation are quite familiar. I do not write as an authority on the subject of a daughter choosing to live at home—I write as a sister in Christ, a peer and a co-laborer, one who still has so much to learn.

As a peer, I want to encourage young women to see stay-at-home daughterhood, not just as a viable option, not as second-best to other things they could have chosen, not as something they need to apologize for, not as an excuse for laziness or a directionless attitude, but as a way to minister in and through the home.

I want to encourage young women to shift their focus, to turn their hearts towards the home, to be enthusiastic and vibrant, purposeful and driven, meticulous and passionately focused in pursuit of the Lord's will for their time at home. I want them to grasp the bigger picture: A vision for the home as a hub of ministry and discipleship, as a training ground for life ahead, as a place where they can bless those nearest and dearest to them, and, as a result, turn that blessing outward towards others in their church and community.

If you are just now coming home, full of fire and passion, I want to encourage you to keep it up! You are doing amazing work for the kingdom. If you have been home for a while, and you find your passion derailed as you look for a fresh perspective on your home life, God bless you—I want to try to give you that perspective. If you aren't a stay-at-home daughter, and you are curious about what this "home girl" thing is all about, I hope this book will give you an opportunity to see into the heart of a daughter living at home, and I pray that what you find there is my passion for the Lord, and for encouraging other young women to live joyfully for him.

This book will be divided into four sections. In the first section, I will focus on the ways to stay joyful at home in the physical sense. I want to encourage you to relate to your father, mother, and siblings in a Christ-honoring way, and to view the family unit as a spiritual boot camp. In the second section, I will focus on how we can stay joyfully content at home, putting our romantic aspirations in proper perspective. In the third section, I will focus on how we can joyfully answer difficult questions about why we are living at home. And, finally, I will focus on how we can turn that homeward vision outward, using these single years under our fathers' roofs to bless the church and the community.

All that being said, as this journey gets underway, it is my prayer that this book will encourage and challenge you, and inspire you to encourage and challenge others as you strive to live *joyfully* for Christ in your own home.

Part One

CHAPTER ONE

Becoming a Good Daughter to Your Heavenly Father

Our Chief End

Before we can learn about being good daughters or good sisters—before we can talk about becoming good wives or training to be godly mothers—before we can talk about using our gifts, talents, and abilities to bless those in the amazing sphere of the home . . .

We have to understand that, as believers, the chief end of all of these pursuits—and of every other pursuit we could think to undertake—is the same: In the words of the Westminster Shorter Catechism, man's primary purpose is to glorify God and enjoy him forever.[1]

It doesn't take much searching to realize that, in our post-modern culture, and because of our sin-natures (Psalm 51:5), making decisions for the glory of God and not for the gratification of our flesh is not an easy task. But because we have been redeemed by the blood of Christ (2 Corinthians 5:17), and because we have a flawless road map in the Word of God (2 Timothy 3:16-17), we are capable of taking the road less traveled (Matthew 7:13-14) and re-examining our presuppositions based on the wisdom of God's Word (2 Corinthians 10:5).

The book you hold in your hands only has merit insofar as it encourages you to delve deeper into the Word of God as you grow into the young woman that he has called you to be.

However, knowing where to start can be daunting. Knowing which voices to listen to in the din of conflicting opinions can be confusing! If we want to get a solid grasp on biblical womanhood, where do we start?

We Start with the Gospel

Here's what I love about God's Word (and there are, of course, many other things I love as well): I love seeing God's redemptive play playing out from Genesis to Revelation—from the promise the Lord made Adam and Eve in Genesis 3:15—to his preservation of the godly seed through Abraham, Isaac, Jacob, and later, David—to the birth of Jesus Christ in Bethlehem—to his death at Calvary—to his Ascension and the promise of his return—to the fulfilling of that promise as revealed in Revelation, which we wait for with hope.

The whole of God's Word points to Jesus Christ—all of it heralds that gospel message. It's the story of a loving God who provides for his people again and again. And it's the story of a wayward people who are ransomed by the blood of God's own Son. We are saved, not by our own merits, but by the grace of God (Ephesians 2). We are saved for his glory, to take part in his redemptive plan, which is constantly playing out through history.

Does this salvation have any impact on us? Or do we continue to walk in the flesh? Are we ransomed children of God to live our lives with the same hedonistic focus that is hard-wired in our hearts since birth—or have we been given a new heart (Psalm 51)? Do we walk in the patterns of this world (Romans 1), or do we now walk in the patterns of righteousness (Romans 6)?

The answer came again and again during our church's study in Romans last month: *Our righteousness does not produce grace*—grace is the free gift of God—but righteousness is a result of the grace that the Lord lavished—and continues to lavish—on our lives (Romans 4:1-8).

As cherished daughters of the Most High, we are now able to spend every day in pursuit of our primary purpose: To glorify God, and to enjoy him forever.

How Can We Glorify God?

My brother Trey and I did not grow up learning catechism, although we were always taught the importance of Scripture memorization. When my brother Elijah first started talking (he is fourteen years younger than I, and eleven years younger than Trey), Daddy introduced us (we were about thirteen and sixteen at the time, respectively) to the children's catechism as well as the Westminster Shorter Catechism. Because the children's catechism is so fresh on my mind, every time I hear certain questions—"What is justification?" "For whom did Christ die?" "What is the first commandment?"—the lines of the children's catechism flood to my mind.

Such is the case with the question, "How can we glorify God?"

I can hear my six-year-old brother lisping through three missing teeth, and my three-year-old brother eagerly replying, "By loving him and doing what he commands."[2]

I can also hear the question preceding it, "Why did God make you and all things?"

Answer: "For his glory."

We are to love the Lord and cherish his commands (Ecclesiastes 12:13; Mark 12:29-31; John 15:8-10; 1 Corinthians 10:31)—our steps are to be guided by his precepts, not our own desires.

When we look into God's Word for his plan for his daughters—as we move forward to apply Scriptural principles to our lives, our chief end must be our primary focus—and the way to carry out that chief end is to love the Lord with all of our hearts, our souls, and our minds (Matthew 22:37) and to do what he commands (1 John 3:4-10).

So What Does God Command of Daughters?

On the most basic level, he commands of his daughters the same thing that he commands of his sons. We do not have blue and pink Bibles, after all, with the Great Commission given to men and the Kitchen Commission given to women. As God's children, we are all commanded to serve him with every gift, talent, and ability that we possess, with a view towards loving him with our whole hearts, serving the brethren, and advancing the gospel to unbelievers (Mathew 22:27-39, 18:19ff).

However, the Lord *did* create us "male and female" for a reason. As women, we were created with distinct, complementary differences from the men in our lives. This has less to do with placing women in a position of inferiority than it does with the fact that we serve a God of order. Even the account of Eve's creation reveals distinctions between male and female.

In one section of his book, *Evangelical Feminism and Biblical Truth*, Dr. Wayne Grudem gives ten arguments that prove male headship in a marriage before the fall:

The *order*: Adam was created first, then Eve (note the sequence in Genesis 2:7 and 2:18-23; 1 Timothy 2:13).

The *representation*: Adam, not Eve, had a special role in representing the human race (1 Corinthians 15:22, 45-49; Romans 5:12-21).

The *naming of woman*: Adam named Eve; Eve did not name Adam (Genesis 2:23).

The naming of the human race: God named the human race "Man," not "Woman" (Genesis 5:2).

The *primary accountability*: God called Adam to account first after the Fall (Genesis 3:9).

The *purpose*: Eve was created as a helper for Adam, not Adam as a helper for Eve (Genesis 2:18; 1 Corinthians 11:9).

The *conflict*: The Curse brought a distortion to previous roles, not the introduction of new roles (Genesis 3:16).

The *restoration*: Salvation in Christ in the New Testament reaffirms the creation order (Colossians 3:18-19).

The *mystery*: Marriage from the beginning of creation was a picture of the relationship between Christ and the church (Ephesians 5:32-33).

The *parallel with the Trinity*: The equality, differences, and unity between men and women reflect the equality, difference, and unity in the Trinity (1 Corinthians 11:3.)[3]

The apostle Paul gives a beautiful illustration of the complementary relationships of a man and his wife in Ephesians 5:22ff—the importance of fully understanding the dynamics of this relationship is magnified when we realize that the relationship between a man and his wife is an illustration of the relationship between Christ and his church! When we are not following God's purpose for marriage, we are presenting the world with a false picture of his relationship with his Bride.

Because a debate about egalitarianism and complementarianism is outside of the scope of this particular book, I direct you to Grudem's excellent analysis of the concept in the work I just cited.

What Does Feminism Have to Do with It?

Feminism is poisonous.

It's a notion that you may have heard before. Feminism is the big bad wolf—it's the wicked witch of the West—it's the boogeyman.

If feminism was simply the notion that women are of equal worth to men, it would be something I supported wholeheartedly. As a Christian woman, I believe that cherishing God's Word would lead us to stand against abuse for either gender. But, also, as Christians, we need to be aware of the dangerous side of feminism: Egalitarianism, for instance, or the idea that men and women are interchangeable. Androgyny—the eradication of gender lines. A sense of entitlement—saying "I deserve this or that" or "I am woman, hear me roar!" instead of leaning humbly on the Lord and His Word when it comes to defining who we are and what we deserve. Sexism—the sneaky idea that women are of more value than the messy, awkward, mentally inferior, and naturally chauvinistic men in their lives. Defensiveness—the idea that women have to fight for their rights because men are hard-wired to dominate and abuse them. In the sense that feminism encourages women to buck the roles given them in God's Word, it *is* dangerous, to marriages, to families, and to femininity and womanhood themselves.

I know, this is not a popular notion. As a young, American woman, I have been told time and again how thankful I ought to be for feminism: It has given me the right to vote and own property; it has given me protection from an abusive marriage; it has given me options beyond the scope of the Susie Homemaker mold that women before the rise of feminism have been forced into! Women before the dawn of feminism had it bad. Right, guys?

However, I have found that, when it comes to talking about the triumphs of feminism, many of us are guilty of giving heed to what C.S. Lewis once called "chronological snobbery." Lewis discusses this phenomenon in his book, *Surprised by Joy:*

> *Barfield never made me an Anthroposophist, but his counterattacks destroyed forever two elements in my own thought. In the first place he made short work of what I have called my "chronological snobbery," the uncritical acceptance of the intellectual climate common to our own age and the*

assumption that whatever has gone out of date is on that account discredited. You must find why it went out of date. Was it ever refuted (and if so by whom, where and how conclusively) or did it merely die away as fashions do? If the latter, this tells us nothing about its truth or falsehood. From seeing this, one passes to the realization that our own age is also a "period," and certainly has, like all periods, its own characteristic illusions. They are likeliest to lurk in those widespread assumptions which are so ingrained in the age that no one dares to attack or feels it necessary to defend them.[4]

Feminism has changed things. Yes, and it has been changing things for much longer than the first or second wave of feminism. It has been changing things since Eve bucked the Lord's natural order and ate of the forbidden fruit (Genesis 3). While it can be very easy to look through the annals of history through our twenty-first century eyes and paint the world before the rise of organized feminism as a dark, dank place where women were systematically mistreated and abused by their male counterparts, a careful reading of history would tell us otherwise. Although, before the dawn of our modern egalitarian leanings, women and men occupied completely different roles in society, we have the legacies of women like Abigail Adams, Sarah Edwards, Anne Bradstreet, and others to show us that this position was not one of mental or spiritual inferiority, but one of order.

In an effort to correct chronological snobbery, we have to be careful not to let the pendulum swing too far in the opposite direction—there is no "ideal" time period. Our sovereign Lord chose for us to occupy this time in history, not so we could crane our necks back in the past for better things—sin has run rampant in every era since the Fall—but so that we can look to God's Word and look forward to the coming of Christ as we carry out the tasks he has given us.

Still, where do single women fit into this understanding of mankind? Though a hierarchy in marriage may seem ordered enough to you, even the most die-hard complementarians often shrug their shoulders when it comes to how unmarried women fit into our understanding of male/female distinctions. While young men and married men are both trained to be leaders and providers in society, oftentimes, young women are trained in the same pattern as young men, and then told that, once they marry, they are given a different role to occupy.

Is God's Word Silent?

Sometimes it may seem that the Word of God is silent when it comes to the issue of a single woman's calling. The primary reason might be that young women often resided in their fathers' households until they were married (Numbers 30, Deuteronomy 22), and were given in marriage by their fathers' (Jeremiah 29:6). For a woman my age—and the age of many of the young ladies reading this book—to still be single in biblical times would be an anomaly.

For a woman my age to be single fifty years ago would have been seen by many as an anomaly as well.

Because of our current state of prolonged singleness, and because of the cultural shift we have seen over the past few decades as feminism has gained a stronger hold on our presuppositions, when it comes to adult daughters finding a purpose in life that lines up with the biblical pattern for women—we are completely lost.

Should we focus our time and energy into building a career and sowing character traits that will align us more and more with the androgynous dream of success and happiness that the culture has laid before us? Should we follow unbelieving young women in lockstep, in hopes of competing with them for the same goals and aspirations? Should we train ourselves to be what my dad calls "men who are biologically capable of having children" during our single years, in the vain hope that the same character qualities that we are sowing in our single lives won't carry over into matrimony—that once we say "I do," the submissive, gentle and quiet spirit that the Lord so prizes in his daughters (1 Peter 3:1-6) will miraculously manifest itself in a field where it has not been patiently cultivated?

I say *no*. And I say it in one voice with hundreds of other young women who have decided to be the anti-feminist trailblazers of the next generation. Most importantly, I believe that I say it in one voice with the purposes that the Lord has laid out in His Word.

As you plan for your future, do so with the beauty of biblical womanhood as your focus, cultivating the beautiful attributes of the Proverbs 31 woman as you seek to bless and spur on others to godliness in the sphere where the Lord has placed you, bringing a hearty femininity to your surroundings, wherever they may be.

Is Being a Stay-at-Home Daughter the Answer?

Stay-at-home daughterhood—the practice of living at home, under your father's authority and parental discipleship until marriage—was normative during biblical times. While the passages that talk about daughters in this context are limited in God's Word, they certainly seem to point to the biblical validity of staying home more than they do to striking out on your own. However, it is difficult to make a case that *not* staying at home between graduation from high school and marriage is a sin. Moreover, because of the fallen world we live in, for many young women, stay-at-home daughterhood in the sense that I will be talking about it in this book is an impossibility because of your family situation.

This book is not about constructing a superficial list of do's and don't's for daughters. It isn't about giving you the one-two-threes of living a perfect life. It isn't about falling into a cookie-cutter mold as a Christian daughter. I do not promise that reading this book will ensure everlasting happiness and unwavering contentment. Because we live east of Eden—because we occupy a fallen world—perfect circumstances are impossible. However, because we have victory through Jesus Christ, fruitful obedience to his commands and the joyful application of biblical principles to our lives is certainly possible—and profitable—and commanded.

Stay-at-home daughterhood is a biblical option that I believe all Christian young women should consider, given the principles of biblical womanhood, and given the responsibility of fathers for the protection of their daughters.

Now, just because I believe all daughters should consider it does not mean that all daughters will decide to pursue it. There will be broken homes where stay-at-home daughterhood is not an option. There will be daughters who submit to their parents by leaving the home. There will be different paths taken. There will be daughters who *do* consider stay-at-home daughterhood . . . and then decide to pursue a different path. There will be hang-ups. There will be daughters who would love to stay-at-home . . . except for *this* or *that*. There will be daughters who choose to serve the Lord in other ways.

However, the simple statement that stay-at-home daughterhood was something that I should consider changed my path five years ago. The more I have grown in grace, the more I have benefited from this environment, the more I have delved into God's Word, the more I am convinced that I will never look back.

Exceptions, different paths, or hang-ups aside, the most important thing I want you to take from this book is to search God's Word, and not the dictates of the culture around you, for your path and for your answers, and to live, unapologetically, the convictions you develop by doing so. Be willing to let God's Word challenge your presuppositions.

Ending with the Gospel

I've brought you full circle in this chapter because I thought it was important to begin at the beginning. The only way to have fruitful at-home years is to have a fruitful relationship with Jesus Christ. This relationship cannot be something that you are simply borrowing from your mom and dad, or something that you know to be true, but that you do not live out, day by day, in your walk. And it cannot be something that you are not willing to give your life for.

If you are not the daughter of the King of Kings, you will not be an effective daughter of your earthly parents. If you are not a sister of God's children, you will not be a good sister to the brothers and sisters in your household. If you are not an ambassador of Christ, your lifestyle cannot witness to the dying world around you.

If the Lord Jesus Christ has not transformed you (Romans 12:1-2), you are not capable of walking in the righteousness to which he has called you (Romans 1:18-20). If you are not being constantly sanctified, daily striving to walk by the spirit (Galatians 5:22ff), you will fall into the deeds of the flesh (Galatians 5:19-21).

You can try your hardest to be a faithful daughter, but if you are trying in your own power, apart from the saving grace of Jesus Christ, you will fail, and your works will be empty and meaningless (Romans 3:28). Conversely, you can profess Jesus Christ with every bit of energy that you have, but if your profession is not followed with the fruit of righteousness, it is meaningless (James 2:24-26).

Are you saved? Do you know the Most High God? Do you understand the depths of his glory, the beauty of his sacrifice for the ransomed? Are you redeemed?

If the answer to any of those questions is no, I beg you to turn to him, and to understand that, without saving faith in Jesus Christ, your quest to become a good daughter is as meaningless as your quest to be a good person without him.

Starting Off on the Right Foot

If, however, you are a daughter of the Most High, it is important for you to surround yourself with things that will constantly bring your focus in line with his purpose for you: his glory. The first way to stay joyful at home is to find your joy in being God's daughter.

As you strive to become the woman that the Lord has called you to be, strive to cultivate the virtues that he has deemed lovely, and strive to maintain a heavenly focus in your every endeavor.

With all of this said, as we dig into family relationships in the next few chapters and reach beyond those relationships in the discussions to follow, I pray that a love for the Lord and his precepts will color everything else you read in this book!

CHAPTER TWO

Becoming a Good Daughter to Your Mother

Titus 2:3-5 says: "Older women likewise are to be reverent in behavior, not slanderers or slaves to much wine. They are to teach what is good, and so train the young women to love their husbands and children, to be self-controlled, pure, working at home, kind, and submissive to their own husbands, that the word of God may not be reviled."

In Search of Titus 2

I have heard so many conversations between young married women who are sighing, "I wish I knew a Titus 2 woman who could walk alongside me! I have so much to learn!"

They talk about how they were trained to have a career, but not to run a home; how they could oversee a business merger, but couldn't manage dinner; how they could juggle nine tasks at once, as long as none of those tasks included the difficulties of child-rearing.

As I sit here typing today, working on my first book and babysitting a six-year-old, a three-year-old, and a two-year-old, I can only imagine the overwhelmed feeling that is sending many a new wife and mommy reeling. My youngest brother Micah (a year old) will be up from nap soon, ready to eat. My three-year-old brother Asher is insatiably curious, and has me running outside every few minutes to answer his plaintive knocks at the door. The two-year-old (Judah) will need a diaper change soon, and it will probably have a smell that would send you running for the hills. Elijah is the oldest of the younger set, and he knows how to keep things in order. The only problem is, this little guy isn't exactly seen as an authority in his toddler brothers' lives.

So how am I not screaming my head off or running for cover?

To be honest with you, sometimes, I would most certainly like to. But I'm capable of handling what could turn into a madhouse not because I'm a zookeeper at heart, but because 1) my parents have diligently trained all of my brothers, and 2) because I have the Titus 2 trainer so many women are looking for.

Many of us have been blessed with a "Titus 2" mentor living under the same roof. I know I have. My mother is, undoubtedly, the person who I spend the most time with. Ever since I can remember, even during difficult seasons of growth, I've been trailing behind her, helping her around the house, hopping in the passenger seat when she runs to do errands, swinging my legs over the side of the bathtub while she's getting ready, talking the whole way, telling her *everything*, asking her *anything*, and being ever-constantly discipled.

My friends have gotten used to asking me for advice and hearing, "Well, here's what I think . . . but I really need to ask my mama, and I'll get back to you." They've probably grown tired of hearing, in response to, "Can you keep a secret?" "Not from my mama" or "Don't tell me anything I can't tell my mama." And they've grown accustomed to me sometimes turning down invitations: "Well, that sounds like fun, but I was going to spend the day with my mama."

Don't get me wrong: I love my friends, and I'm going to talk about godly friendships in another section of the book; but my relationship with my mother is special.

Though I've gotten a bit too big to swing my legs over the side of that tub, I've taken over some of the chores I used to help with, and now I cart *Mama* in the passenger's seat for errands, our relationship has deepened over the years. My mother is the Proverbs 31 woman in action; she is the person who's kindest redirection can bring me to my knees in repentance, or who's slightest change in expression can double me over in laughter.

Now, there's only one Bridget Baucham, and she's mine (well . . . technically, she's my dad's, but . . . you know what I mean.) But if you want to learn about biblical womanhood, most often, you don't have to look any further than the woman of the house. Spend time with your mother. Hearken to your mother. Honor your mother. Serve your mother.

Our mamas are all less than perfect, because we're all fallible humans. There is an old saying, "Familiarity breeds contempt." Although few of us would say that we feel *contempt* for either of our parents, many of us are so used to concentrating on our mothers' faults (on the things we dislike about her, on the pet-peeves we have cultivated, on the daily annoyances we can so easily become hung up on, on the character flaws we have grown up noticing, etc.). We tend to be far less patient with our mothers than we ought to be; however, as we show forbearance and as we learn to focus, not on the flaws we see in our mothers, but, instead, on their virtues, many of us will realize that we are living with Proverbs 31 women that we have not even learned to appreciate.

Every family is a tool of sanctification and sharpening. Mothers have insights about us that even *we* never suspected! And even as I've grown older, and even though I've learned to "think for myself," I still believe that, in most cases, mama knows best—even when obeying her wisdom doesn't come easily for us.

But What Does that *Look* Like?

But really, practically, what does this relationship look like? So often, I have found that the best way to describe what a loving relationship with your mother looks like is to let you know what it *doesn't* look like. An excellent catalyst for this discussion came in the form of an inquiry I received several months ago through my blog:

> *Hi Jasmine!*
>
> *So, the first time I found out that your dad actually even had a daughter my age (I'm 20) was when I watched* Return of the Daughters. *(Which I love, btw. :)*
>
> *I have tried to become more supportive of my parents' vision as a result of convictions springing from the documentary . . . (I was already a stay at home daughter and all) . . . and to be a helper to my dad. Which usually goes over pretty well since my dad and I are very alike, have the same "love languages" etc.*
>
> *So my question comes here.*

*My mom started to feel a little "jealous" because she felt like
I was taking her spot of helping my dad, making his favorite
foods, walking next to him while shopping, and all of that.*

And that began my wondering . . .

*How can I be a loving helper to my dad when my mom is his
true help-meet and he is designed to only have one, and I am
designed to have my own man to support and help but (in God's
timing) he hasn't showed up yet?*

*Maybe this is a somewhat unusual question, but I do desire to
have good family harmony and help my parents (my spiritual gift
is serving). . . I really appreciated what you had to say in* Return
of the Daughters, *so wondered if you had any insights for me.*

In all honesty, I was ecstatic to have the opportunity to answer what had
been mentioned as a deep concern in the "stay at home daughter movement:"
What about the mothers? In their book, *So Much More*, Anna and Sofia and
Elizabeth Botkin offer incredible insight into the father/daughter relationship.
Yet they write:

*Is [a daughter's] missing relationship with [her father] the root
of all [her] problems? No, not the only root. But we believe
after years of studying both God's Word and modern times, that
the forgotten principles of fatherly protection and daughterly
honor are the missing dynamic girls need in leading fruitful,
stable, happy lives which will give honor to God. We do not
believe that the father-daughter relationship is somehow more
important or special than the mother-daughter relationship,
or the father-son relationship, nor do we mean to breath into
this relationship some kind of super-special, mystical quality
never seen in the Bible. But we do believe the father-daughter
relationship is one of those being more ignored and abused [in]
this generation than others, with disastrous and heartbreaking
repercussions. Girls are hurting from the absence of strong,
biblical relationships with their fathers, and repairing things
should be a priority for young women in our generation.*[5]

I for one give a hearty amen to that assessment. Now, I do believe it is
possible to overcorrect, making the pendulum swing so far in the opposite
direction that we knock mothers completely out of the picture. While this
is something I saw nowhere advocated in *So Much More*, I have seen an

increasing number of young women living at home who, instead of benefiting from the tutelage of their mothers at home, are constantly jockeying for their mother's household responsibilities, so anxious to learn and to grow and to help that they miss the bigger picture: Benefiting from the Titus 2 mentorship of the most important woman in their lives.

Your Parents' Relationship is the Most Important Thing

When my daddy comes home from an out-of-town trip, though the boys squeal and clamor next to the front door as soon as they hear the garage, all of us kids know that Daddy's first priority when he enters the house isn't going to be to scoop one of us up in a bear hug or tousle our hair. Daddy will walk into the house, his eyes searching, looking right past his children. He will part the clamoring crowd and make a beeline for Mama. And only after he's said his hellos to her (sometimes making us gag playfully in the process) will he turn around and greet us enthusiastically.

It's something we kids are used to, and something that, as we grow up, we learn to love. From a very young age, my parents have made it apparent that their relationship supersedes everything else in our family life.

If we are going to live in harmony at home with our families, finding the balance between walking as an adult while still being our mother and fathers' daughter, the first thing we need to remember is that our parents' marriage is the most important relationship at home.

Their marriage is the foundation upon which your family is built, and it's only because of their healthy marriage that we can have healthy homes. My daddy may be the head of his wife, and of his household, but when it comes to us kids, we are under both of our parents' authority. If we're doing anything to undermine that relationship, we're undermining our family dynamic in a crippling fashion. As their children, we need to understand that we should be encouraging our parents in their pursuit of a godly marriage, not doing anything to hinder that pursuit. We know that a strong marriage is the stepping stone to a strong family unit, and that the relationships within that unit are what defines a strong family. We have to work to keep every relationship running smoothly—biblically.

Now, a strong mother and father who realize the importance of their relationship will be quick to let us know when we've gotten out of line. And, when they do, our response should be brokenness and repentance. "But what if I was just trying to help my father, and by doing so, better learn how to help my future spouse?" You know what will really help you serve your future spouse? Observing the union of your parents; they are as one, not to be divided by our overzealous efforts to help dad (or, in other ways: by us making snide remarks about one parent to the other, or running to one parent when another says or does something we don't like, to name a couple of examples).

Setting Boundaries

As we learn the importance of the marriage relationship, adult daughters will need to establish strong boundaries by respecting both of their parents. The first way to set boundaries is to *listen*. When your mother says that she'd rather accomplish a chore, do not clamor to relieve her of it; step aside. As you seek to become a woman of God, one of the best things that you can do is to honor the Proverbs 31 woman in your life by submitting yourself to her authority.

Before you think to do something for your dad, ask your mom what her plans are. She is your father's helpmeet, not you, and that's a role that you should honor. Do things to show your mother that you recognize her place in the home, and that you understand that it is not your calling to usurp that place. And do things to show her that you appreciate Mom and Dad, and the importance of their relationship.

Something I like to do to show my mama that I care for her is to hint around to my dad when I think of something she might enjoy. My dad's pretty romantic all on his own, but sometimes, I'll run across something to suggest to him. Several months ago, I saw an advertisement for a play I knew my mom would love. I booked the play and ran downstairs to show daddy that I'd found them front row seats at a great price, if they were interested. Of course he was (and later bought season tickets, just for the two of them). The night of the play—just like I try to do whenever my parents go out together—I assured them that I was completely willing to babysit the kids, and that they should stay out as late as they wanted and to have a great time.

Every once in a while, you might let your mom know you're always available if she wants to do something special with your dad, that she doesn't have to worry about the house while she's gone (sometimes, for my parents, this can even mean a week-long vacation), that you'll take care of everything so they can be together. It doesn't have to be something as big as that. When you see your mom and dad sitting and talking on the couch, even if it's just a leisurely conversation, you can gather your siblings and take them to another room to play quietly so your parents can have some down time together. It's a little thing, but it shows that you care.

Helping Dad and Mom

It's important to remember that you have two parents, and both have a very important role in your discipleship. Your father's role is to protect and guide you, and he is the head of your household, yes, but your mother holds an equally important role as your example of Proverbs 31 and as your Titus 2 mentor. Having a good relationship with both of our parents should be a priority.

It is important to help where you are needed, which sometimes means helping in a way that would not be your first choice. If your mom's helping your dad with a project, your job isn't to push her out of the way, but to find something else to do. This may be something to help your mom, or even something to help a lady in your neighborhood or in your church. Can you start a home business? Can you babysit or teach piano lessons? Your mom might not have enough time to do more tedious office work for your dad; maybe that's something you can take care of. Your mom and dad may need to go and minister to someone in the church. Perhaps you can go grocery shopping for your mom that day. We can make a point to cook a couple of meals a week for our mom, to organize our dad's paperwork, or any number of things, but we need to make sure that what we're doing is really an asset to our parents before we forge ahead.

How it works out for me is that I'm my dad's research assistant, but I have to balance that with my other responsibilities; most of my time is actually spent helping my mom with the boys, with the errands, and with the household chores. I try to tackle the things that will free both of my parents for more important pursuits, like spending time together. Our goal as stay-at-home daughters should be to help the whole home run smoothly, not just to focus in on one parent; it should also be to develop a well-rounded arsenal of tools that will help you down the line as a wife and mother. My job isn't to be my dad's primary helper, and it's not a position I'm vying for, because I understand that my best preparation for being a wife and mom comes from understanding that both of my parents play a pivotal role in that process.

Having a Good Relationship with Both Parents

Do you know your mom's favorite color? Do you know just what to get her for her birthday? Do you know what movie to pop into the DVD player when she wants to relax? What kind of music does she love?

It's important for us girls to get to know our daddies, and to show affection to them as well—that's something that seriously lacking in our day and age. Instead of developing fruitful relationships with our fathers, we're looking for affirmation in all of the wrong places.

However, in righting this wrong, we cannot ignore our mothers, who are of equal importance. My mom is my favorite person to be with. It wasn't always the case. I've always been much more like my father. However, as I've grown to truly appreciate the woman of God that my mother is, and the wonderful opportunity I have to learn from her during these years at home, a new closeness has grown between us. What made it hard during those adolescent years wasn't a personality difference at all, but a misunderstanding of who she was in my life.

I had a career-woman mentality from a young age (twelve going on twenty-two), and didn't think I had anything to learn from my mom. Boy, was I wrong! And I'm glad I was! The more I got to know my mom, the more I realized that both of my parents had shaped my character; yes, I'm more like my dad, but my mom and I have things in common, too! And Daddy is no good with girl talk. We work together, we talk together, we laugh together, and I learn so much from her example, and I wouldn't trade her for anything. At the risk of gushing, I have to say that our relationship is one of the most important in my life. I think that if young women are too busy butting heads with their mothers over who's going to do what household chore, they are not only dishonoring the Lord by undermining their mothers' authority, but also missing out on a crucial opportunity to nurture a relationship with their moms.

The Goal

If we want to use this time in our lives to take advantage of the opportunity for discipleship and service in our home, we need to remember our primary goal: To glorify the Lord. In looking towards that purpose, we need to realize that our motive in acts of service and our drive to become the women the Lord has called us to be needs to come from a zeal for the Lord. Our parents have been given to us to guide, protect, and disciple us as we walk this path. In respecting both of our parents, in serving them both, in walking alongside them both— our mothers as they demonstrate godly womanhood for us to mirror, our fathers as they demonstrate the biblical manhood that we're looking for in a husband—our goal is to please the Lord.

Our time for wifehood will come soon enough—God's timing is perfect. But this season of daughterhood is pivotal for our spiritual development. We mustn't become myopic in our focus; the big picture presents an inspiring reality: As single ladies, we have a unique opportunity to serve during this time in our lives. We must make sure that our acts of service are pleasing to the

Lord, and we must act in submission to both of our parents, and be careful not to let ourselves become overzealous to the point that we lose sight of our place in the home. The headstrong independence that we claim to have gotten rid of in order to better serve our families is just directed a little differently. Now, instead of wanting to skyrocket in a law firm, we sometimes try to control every aspect of our homes instead of taking a backseat. The sin is still there—it just has a different name. Once we learn how to rein it in (or rather, once we submit to our authorities, and submit to the Father, and he graciously reins it in), the opportunities for truly blessing others are limitless.

And remember, supporting your dad's vision means his vision for the entire family; those goals can be met even when you're not directly helping your father; anything you do for your family, or as your family's ambassador to others, under the direction of your parents, can be furthering your dad's vision.

One woman at our church used to joke that if a daughter is anyone's helpmeet-in-training, it should be her mother's. Now, taken to the theological extent, this assessment is a little *too* bold; but what she was saying in her famously roundabout way was that if you are a stay-at-home daughter, most of your time is going to be spent with your mom.

Cultivate a good relationship with her by sharing your heart with her, and knowing her heart—by blessing her through acts of service and obedience—by working *with* her to keep the house running smoothly, not without her—and by thanking the Lord every single day for a mom who can lead you diligently in his ways.

Thank the Lord, also, for a father who can lead your mother and your family in the Lord's ways as well. Our relationship with our mothers is only half of the picture when it comes to bringing harmony to your home. In the next chapter, I hope to encourage you to cultivate a fruitful relationship with your father as well.

CHAPTER THREE

Becoming a Good Daughter to Your Father

I was born a Daddy's girl. Although my mama was the one that carried me for nine months, she used to joke that she was just cooking up Dad's clone. I happen to look just like my father, and our personalities are incredibly similar. When I was a baby, I slept on the twenty-one-year-old's chest just about every night; when I was a toddler, I trailed him everywhere; when I started school, I wanted to be smart "just like Daddy."

I was always talking to him about the things that were near and dear to my heart. My dad and I had heart-to-hearts about theological truths. I could always come to him when I had a question about something I was learning in God's Word, or even when I was struggling to understand a conviction that I knew he held, but couldn't quite understand for myself. We also talked about my friends. I asked my dad about advice I ought to give my peers, or better ways to relate to others. As I started getting older, the thing we most talked about was college. I had big dreams, and my dad had high expectations, and the older I got, the more visionary we both became about the subject.

I have always loved my dad, and always enjoyed his company. But I did not always understand exactly the role he had been called to play in my life.

Your Dad as a Protector

Daddy has always protected me. He was the tight end in Rice University's football team right before I was born, and it shows. I remember the first time I realized my dad was an imposing figure. I was coming out to the car after a day at my homeschool co-op, and a male friend of mine was following behind me, asking about a homework assignment. Daddy got out of the car when he saw us coming, and smiled warmly at my friend.

"Joe, this is dad! Dad, Joe!" I said, grinning as they shook hands, noting how Joe stuttered out the words. "So nice to meet you, Mr. Baucham."

"Hey, Daddy." I smiled, leaning in for a hug from my dad before running back to the car. "See you next week!" I called back to my friend who stood dazed on the sidewalk.

"I don't want you talking to Aggies," Daddy joked, taking note of my friend's maroon Texas A&M University shirt as we pulled out of the parking lot. Joe just stood there as we pulled off, staring.

Next week, I asked Joe why he had acted so weird around my father. He looked at me with huge eyes. "Yeah, duh—your dad is huge!"

I just laughed. I hadn't noticed, but, as I got a little older, I started to realize that Joe wasn't the only guy who had. The joke around class became, "Don't mess with Jasmine! Her dad was an all-American!"

Aside from his imposing stature, my dad also has somewhat of a reputation in evangelical circles. As a long-time itinerant preacher who is also an elder at a family integrated church in the Houston area and author of three (soon to be four) books and a Bible study, Daddy doesn't like to toot his own horn—but I gladly toot it on his behalf. I'm used to wide-eyed spectators mooning, "You're Voddie Baucham's daughter?" and I'm used to being referred to as "Voddie's Daughter," as if that's the name on my birth certificate. So if it wasn't Daddy's football physique that made my male friends nervous, books like, *What He Must Be*, have often done the trick.

However, as blessed as I am and have always been by the amazing man my dad is and has been since I was a little girl—on the football field, in the college classroom, behind the podium at events that reach one hundred thousand listeners a year, and as the loving shepherd in our home—it never occurred to me growing up how serious his responsibility was as my protector.

If your dad loves the Lord, you have been given an incredible blessing in him. If he strives to instill biblical wisdom in you (Deuteronomy 6, Ephesians 6:1-4), and if he has a vision for your family, you are doubly blessed. You have been given the amazing opportunity to bless your father as he strives to be the priest (Joshua 24:15), prophet (Ephesians 6:4), provider (1 Timothy 5:8; Titus 2:5), and protector (Nehemiah 4:13-14) in your home. You can aid his mission by helping him with his work, taking charge of projects he may have in mind for you, and learning all you can from him about his vision for your family so that you can become an effective ambassador for him outside of your household.

Protection? From What?

As daughters, we also need to graciously cherish our fathers' protection. In a day and age where damsels locked in high towers are no longer held in high esteem, the word needs some defining. It may surprise you to know that the protection of which I speak has little to do with Rapunzel being locked away until her prince can slay the dragon outside the castle walls.

A word like "protector" flies in the face of many of our modern sensibilities. Are stay-at-home daughters allowed outside of their father's sight? Can they go out with friends without a parent present? Are they allowed to have drivers' licenses? Are they allowed to make their own decisions?

As previously stated, the concept of stay-at-home daughterhood is not nearly monolithic enough for me to answer every single one of those questions for every single stay-at-home daughter out there, but I will say, for my part, and for every single stay-at-home daughter that I know, the answer to each of those questions is a resounding *yes*! These are not young women who are caught in the netherworld between childhood and adulthood (their growth retarded by overbearing parents) but competent young women who are investing their energies in their families instead of in a career.

The Proverbs 31 woman traveled away from her home on many occasions (Proverbs 31:10-31), and, as young women, when we do so, we will need to be armed with the skills that will make us competent ambassadors for our families. Being under our father's protection does not give us an excuse to become idle and shiftless, spending every waking moment at home on the couch waiting to be told what to do. On the contrary, it should mean showing initiative and taking charge of the areas our parents delegate to us, branching out on our own projects to further the kingdom, all *under the oversight and guidance of our fathers*.

So when I say I'm under my father's protection, I don't mean that he keeps me on a leash, then what do I mean?

In his book, *God Marriage and Family,*[6] Andreas J. Kostenberger quotes Daniel Block outlining the responsibilities of a father to his daughter in ancient Israel:

- *Protecting his daughter from male "predators" so she would marry as a virgin, thus bringing honor to his name and purity to her husband (cf. Ex. 22:16-17; Deut. 22:13-21)*

- *Arranging for his daughter's marriage by finding a suitable husband and making proper arrangements*

- *Ensuring a measure of security for his daughter by providing a dowry (cf. Gen. 29:24, 29)*

- *Protecting his daughter from rash vows (Num. 30:2-15)*

- *Providing security for his daughter in case the marriage failed; and perhaps also*

- *Instructing his daughter in the Scriptures*[7]

In our day, there is an increasing push to do away with the outdated laws of the Old Testament and to disregard them each in turn as the restrictive rules of a different God than the one we serve. However, Jesus Christ said that he had not come to abolish the Law, but to fulfill it (Matthew 5:17-20). When we read the Old Testament, we have to read it in light of the truth of Jesus Christ. As Saint Augustine is often quoted to have said, "In the old testament the new testament is concealed and in the new testament the old testament is revealed." In other words, these Old Testament responsibilities must be clarified in light of New Testament precepts so we can better understand the *timeless* truths in God's Word.

In his chapter "A Father's Role" from *What He Must Be*, my father uses the example of Numbers 30 to define what we call "gospel patriarchy," or the principle of responsible male headship in the home played out in New Testament life:

> *To interpret the Old Testament in light of the New, we must look at the various marriage texts in the Old Testament through the lens of passages like Ephesians 5. In doing so it is not difficult to see the appropriateness of viewing Numbers 30 in light of Paul's statement that "the husband is the head of the wife even*

as Christ is the head of the church, his body, and is himself its Savior. Now as the church submits to Christ, so also wives should submit everything to their husbands" (Ephesians 5:23-24).

Hence, Numbers 30 is at least about male headship. Fathers are the heads of their households, and as such they 1) represent Christ in the great mystery of marriage, and 2) guide their families in living in accordance to the principles laid out in his word (Ephesians 6:1-4). Hence gospel patriarchs should still be concerned about vows their daughters make to God. The father of a ten-year-old, for example, who declares that God has called her to be a missionary to China can respond, "Instead you ought to say, 'If the Lord wills, we will live and do this or that" (James 4:15).

Moreover, it would be important to take the entire context into account and see this as an exercise of Christlike headship in an effort to purify the bride. In such a case, then Numbers 30 may be applied as follows: Just as Christ protects the purity of his Bride, the husband is called to protect his wife (and his daughters) by helping them avoid hasty decisions (vows). It would be unthinkable for a man to be a passive observer in his household if he takes his role seriously. He is a participant in a living drama played out before a lost, hurting, and dying world that desperately needs to see an accurate picture of the love that Jesus has for his Bride (Ephesians 5:32).[8]

He further states:

Why would God be concerned about the way Old Testament patriarchs prepared their children for marriage but not be concerned about us? Why would he give so much care and attention to the well-being of young women under the Old Covenant but abandon them to laissez-faire fathers under the New? This is inconceivable.

God has not stopped being concerned about fathers leading their daughters into marriage by protecting them from male "predators" so they will marry as virgins; arranging for their marriages by finding a suitable husband and making proper arrangements; ensuring a measure of security for them by providing a form of dowry; protecting them from rash vows; providing security for them if they are abandoned; and doing

all of this at least in part by instructing them in the Scriptures.
Let us go, therefore, and do likewise.[9]

Part of being a good daughter to our fathers is submitting to their protection and guidance in the areas outlined in the Scriptures. We can do this by *seeking their advice in our everyday decisions.* We shouldn't become pests, expecting our busy fathers to have the time to micromanage our every move (part of helping our fathers is being competent enough to do so without constant supervision); however, we should develop a habit of evaluating our decisions as a team.

This is in so many ways counterintuitive in our day. In a time where a potential suitor seeking a daughter's hand in marriage from her father has become no more than an empty tradition that smacks of the same insipidness as roses and chocolates, or a father giving away his blushing daughter at the alter is merely an empty symbol, a daughter who truly submits to her father and delights in his protection is going to be a strange sight.

But it is also a *glorious* sight—a beautiful sight—a biblical sight.

Protecting Your Father's Reputation

As our fathers protect us, we, in turn, must learn how to protect *them.* Because we live at home, there are going to be those who look at our dads in disdain, assuming that we have been *forced* to stay home by the overprotective ogres we call "Daddy." Because of this stereotype, the last thing that we as young women living at home should strive to be is helpless damsels in distress.

How can we protect our fathers' reputations?

One way we can protect our fathers is by *fostering competence* in our characters. We need to be able to take initiative in our homes, and to get things done—to carry out assignments with joy and purpose. This protects our fathers by showing watching eyes that the stereotype of a damsel in distress to be a false one. Helpless damsels have little use in a biblically-functioning home; conscientious daughters are much more helpful.

Another way we can help our dads is by being able to communicate our convictions for ourselves, without having to fall back on, "Because my daddy tells me so." For instance, I once had a friend over, and we were talking about various movies that were playing in the theater at the time. I brought up a movie that I had not seen or read about yet, but was interested in looking into, and my friend—a wonderful, godly nineteen-year-old woman—quipped, "Oh, my dad says I'm not allowed to watch that movie."

When I asked her why, she shrugged her shoulders helplessly. "He just said so." I questioned her further, intent on getting to the bottom of her helpless attitude towards the situation. "Did he say you couldn't ask him *why?*" I wanted to know.

She shook her head. "No. He read something in the paper and said we probably shouldn't be interested in that movie."

"Did he burn the paper afterwards?" I asked.

"No, he left it open on the coffee table."

There is absolutely nothing wrong with a young woman who trusts fully in the wise guidance of her father. However, to do so without caring to seek the reasoning behind the decision might show laziness or indifference on a daughter's part.

We need to understand the rules of our household so that we can better communicate them to those who would ask us. For instance, if you do not have a television, don't shrug your shoulders at a stranger and quip, "My dad doesn't let us watch TV." This paints your father in a negative light—to say that he won't *let* you do something implies that it is something you would like to do, but are being forced not to do. If this is truly how you feel about the situation, I suggest you talk to your father frankly and respectfully, to better understand his position on the matter. If, however, you know your dad's reasoning and agree with his decision, try answering the question like this instead: "We don't watch television. We've found that we can get so much done without that distraction, and I love how we have more time to spend together as a family now." Own your family's convictions.

The first answer is a little girl answer—the second answer is the mature young woman's reply. We need to come to a place where the we own the convictions that have been so patiently instilled in us (Ephesians 6:1-4), where we are not merely parroting or regurgitating what we have heard, but where we are reasoning through our decisions through the grid of God's Word. It needs to be something personal.

To be protected is not to be crippled or hindered in any fashion—to be protected is to have the freedom to bloom in the beautiful environment of the home, under the wise guidance and counsel of your father and mother. A good relationship with both of your parents is a wonderful springboard for spiritual growth. Reason number five hundred and ninety-seven why I love living at home.

Helping Your Father

Many young women have asked me how they can take practical steps to help their fathers. Here are some ways that I have always loved helping my dad: First, I help my dad by **knowing** his vision. I communicate frankly and sincerely with my father about the things that are important to him: cultural apologetics, ethics, family ministry, and, of over-arching importance, the gospel. Because I have taken the time to get to know him, I know the best ways that I can be a blessing to him. Blessedly, because of the similarity in our personalities, my dad and I have been able to work together on several projects—I have worked fulltime as his research assistant, was the online coordinator of his online store for two years before it outgrew the confines of our garage, have written articles for our family newsletter when he didn't have the time to do so, and have recently taken over his booking.

Look around your home. What are some areas where your dad could use a helping hand?

Secondly, I help my dad by **being available** to him. If there is ever anything my dad needs me to do, I try to make time for it. I am constantly questioning him about what he might need from me on a weekly basis, and I make sure to mold my schedule around the things that may be required from me at home. When I was running the online store, there were days when I had to turn down outings with friends because I had fifty messages waiting on my answering machine at home (sometimes, they would come over and help, and we'd make a day of it). I knew that supporting my dad was more important than a trip to the mall.

Third, I **don't wait** for my dad to give voice to practical ways I can help him: I am always looking for them. If I am reading a book that I know will be helpful for some research he's doing, I take notes for him. If I run across an article I think will interest him, I forward it to him. If I am feeling at all directionless, I talk to him about how I can help him with his current projects. Sure enough, even if all he needs is to have the books in his gigantic library re-alphabetized or his office organized, there is always something that I can do.

Finally, I **try not to shy away** from things that he asks me to do. I always try to be up for a new challenge, realizing that part of character growth is doing things that I don't necessarily like to do to aid my dad. For instance, when Daddy needed someone to step in and run the online store, my hand was not the first one to go up. When he asked me to come on as Voddie Baucham Ministries' first and only employee, I was nervous about the huge responsibility. I was relieved when, after it outgrew our garage, the store passed from my hands and into more capable ones, but in the two years that I juggled the store with my other responsibilities, I learned self-discipline that I would not have learned otherwise, and my dad was given aid that he would not have otherwise had.

Owning Your Father's Vision for Your Family

Living at home will give you an opportunity to relate to your father as an adult young woman, seeking his input, treasuring his guidance, and cherishing his protection. I have seen this come to life in my own day-to-day experiences.

What does it mean to cherish your father's provision and protection? Well, it might be easier to start with describing what it is *not*.

To cherish your father's vision is not to wake up every morning and expect him to make your life worthwhile. I have received countless e-mails and inquiries from young women who are throwing up their hands in despair. "My dad doesn't have a vision!" What these girls usually mean is that they are waiting for their fathers to micromanage their time at home, and would feel more comfortable being told what to do every second of every day than actively seeking ways to bless their father and their household on their own.

I have many girls write me to tell me, "Easy for you to say! Your dad has *plenty* of things to keep you busy at home! What about me?"

True enough, I am blessed with a father who constantly needs aid in his ministry, as I am also blessed to be fully invested in what my father is doing, and passionate about his vision for our family.

But if your father is a believer, he also has a vision, and you can easily locate it in God's Word:

> Go therefore and make disciples of all nations, baptizing them in the name of the Father and of the Son and of the Holy Spirit, teaching them to observe all that I have commanded you. And behold, I am with you always, to the end of the age. —Matthew 28:19-21

In that spirit, even if your dad never tells you specific things that you can do to aid him in his vision, you can work on helping him by advancing the gospel in and through your home. Ask your dad if it would be all right if you arranged for two families from your church to come to dinner at your home every week. See if he can spare you once a week to baby-sit for a busy mother at your church. Ask him if it would be all right if you had several younger women over to your family's home one day a week to minister to them.

Most of all, talk to your father about the things of the Lord. Even if he has a difficult time answering your questions, commit to seeking them out with him. If he mentions something that he would like to know, but seems to busy to find it right that second, locate it for him. If he mentions something that he would like you to pursue, look into it.

Again, as daughters, most of us will be spending most of our time working alongside our mothers. As I said in the previous chapter, anything we do to help free our mothers to be better helpmeets to our dad *is* furthering our dad's vision. This includes household chores, errand-running, or child-wrangling.

Many of us, along with being blessed with mothers and fathers, have also been blessed with siblings. And as sanctifying as it is to learn to interact respectfully and productively with our parents, I am convinced that there is no spiritual boot camp quite like learning to relate to our brothers and sisters. In the next chapter, I will discuss some helpful principles that I have learned and applied in my own family life in this area.

CHAPTER FOUR

Becoming a Good Sister to Your Siblings

The Story of Two Distant Siblings

The other day, my brother Trey and I asked Daddy if he had ever known what cool kids we were growing up.

I mean, we two would have fun for hours on end making entire worlds out of Legos, writing songs together to sing in our make-believe boy-band (oh, yes—you read that right; there were five members between the two of us), and writing up shows for our television network and our radio program (the TV shows took place on the trampoline; the radio show was on our tape recorder)—we even wrote our own commercials. Even today, we can recite our Raid commercial from memory, as well as Ma and Pa Bailey's infomercials. Ask us about it sometime—you won't stop laughing. And if you don't happen to giggle, we are sure to fill the quiet spaces by laughing at our own jokes.

One thing we loved to do together while we were living in the UK back in 2000 was to watch superhero cartoons. I loved them. *Spiderman* and *X-Men* shall always have a nostalgic feel for the girl who also loves swing music and classic movies.

It was not until we came back to the States in 2001, when, after plugging in to the local homeschool group and being immersed in the culture of my peer group once more that I realized the stereotype perpetrated by the Disney sitcoms we learned to watch religiously: Little brothers are annoying at best, and sadistic at worse. We are supposed to gripe at them to get out of our rooms, try to hide them when our friends come over, and guard our precious secrets from them lest they spill them to anyone who will listen.

You are not supposed to stay up late giggling with your brother about the events of your day. You are not supposed to be friends with his friends, and enjoy spending time together one-on-one and in a group. You are not supposed to be able to confide in your brother. And you most certainly should not use a spatula or a wooden spoon to burst into an annoying song contest while you're cleaning up the kitchen.

Is it any wonder with rules like these that so many young women have trouble relating to their brothers? Some of us would give anything to mind-read like the superheroes in those comic books of theirs so that we could find out how to get along with them!

Now that I'm a little older, Trey and I still have a host of inside jokes, and I'm convinced we should go on the road with our fantastic comedy routine. I have not felt the need to read his mind in the past ten years or so—Daddy accuses us of twin telepathy every once in a while. But that was not always so. Eleven years ago, you would have had to pay me to spend any amount of time in the same room with my pesky six-year-old brother.

Things changed when my daddy came back from a ministry trip to England and announced, "We're moving to Oxford."

My mother, having lived with a visionary for the past decade, literally nodded and said, "All right."

To this day, I'm not sure if she thought he was joking—but in a matter of months, we were making preparations to move to Oxford, England. It's an adventurous story, one that includes a rather harrowing house hunt (Daddy didn't find a good place for us to stay until just hours before he came home to fetch us), and a rather upset ten-year-old: yours truly.

Call me crazy, but something did not appeal to me about leaving the private school that I'd attended since I was five years old, leaving the friends I had known for just as long, leaving the city I had lived in practically all of my life (minus a year in Fort Worth), leaving the country that I called home, and boarding a half-day flight to the city of many a young girl's daydreams: London.

It was a hard year. We never did find a church home, though we visited several; it was our first year homeschooling, but we didn't plug in to a like-minded co-op; and to my horror, there were only *two* TVs, one downstairs, and a tiny one in Mommy and Daddy's bedroom. I shared a bedroom and a classroom with the little brother who had always annoyed me.

But, away from the distractions of home, our family seemed to be getting to *know* one another for the very first time; we were "forced" to spend time together, to embark on this new adventure, to unite as we had never united before. There were no schoolmates, no Sunday school friends, no events on the weekend; it was just us, the American Bauchams living in a duplex in Oxford. In hindsight, it was a wonderful, blessed, shaping experience, one of the best things that ever happened in my childhood. I got to know my family, and, you know what? I liked them, my brother Trey in particular.

I climbed into the bottom bunk with him during the week that fliers were being passed around about the break-ins in our neighborhood; I played in the sunroom with him when the shorter days had the sun setting at four o' clock in the afternoon; we read out loud to each other in the bedroom we shared for a year; and every night, we watched superhero cartoons I used to refuse to indulge in when we lived in the US. I didn't realize it then, but my brother and I were given the unique opportunity to grow closer to one another than many of the siblings that we knew at the time.

Back in England, I only had one brother. About three years after we settled back into the States, I got another one—three years later, another—nineteen months later, another—a year after that, another. . . . True enough, my love for them is different than my love for Trey—due to the age gap, both Trey and I are a lot more nurturing towards the younger set than we are towards one another, and are naturally inclined to parent them a bit. However, we are all still close, and as I have grown older, and as I have gotten used to this houseful of boys, I've learned a lot about young men and the culture.

The Importance of Brothers

Someday, by God's grace, my brother will be the prophet, priest, provider, and protector in his own home. This was magnified for me while doing research for my father's book *What He Must Be* two years ago. Every time I read a resource, I would think about my brother Trey, and the Lord used that time to impress upon my heart the fact that he could someday be this man. In so many ways, he is becoming a man like the one I pray I will marry.

But, as a man, my brother—and your brother—is fighting against a culture that wants to emasculate him. He is fighting against a culture that makes men afraid to be men, a culture that sees masculinity as something prehistoric, something that has oppressed women since time's dawning, and something that needs to be squelched by sensitivity and psychobabble. As a conservative Christian man who believes that it is his place to take dominion in this ungodly world, guiding his family down the path of righteousness, he already has the culture's cards stacked against him.

So the last thing we need to do as a sister is belittle and invalidate them.

It can be difficult. I am three years older than my brother, and that, coupled with the fact that girls mature faster than boys, and the fact that I am just plain bossy, has shown me that the brother-sister relationship is *such* a huge part of the sanctification process! I have to bite my tongue when I want to nag him about chores; I need to let him lead when Mama and Daddy are gone and there are decisions to be made; I need to encourage him when I see glimpses of that mighty man of God I know he'll become. This will help my oldest brother (and later, my younger four) to recognize his potential. The way I talk to and about him makes an impact! When Trey sees that I'm in his corner, it makes him want to strive to be a better man!

In the same way, I want to encourage you—not to think of your younger brother as a pest; not just to treat him with the same deference you would any other peer, but to love him with the pure, unbridled "one another" love in God's Word (John 15:17, Colossians 3:12-13, 1 Thessalonians 5:11, Hebrews 3:13, etc.). If this is what the Lord commands of the body of believers, how much more for your own brother?

Building up our brothers doesn't just help them to become better men, or give them a place of respite from the battle in the world, but it helps us to become better women. My dad often reminds me that few things can prepare a young woman to submit to her husband better than a teenage girl practicing deference to her teenage brother. No, he is not perfect, but your husband will not be perfect either! Learning to relate to your incredibly flawed brother with gentleness and kindness will instill in you a personality trait that will be invaluable in a marriage.

Isn't it amazing how God built the family unit in such a way that it's impossible to live in it for too long without learning some of life's most important lessons?

A Brief Word about Sisters

By that same token, loving our younger sisters in this fashion can shape them into the godly women the Lord has called them to be. Do you encourage your sisters in righteousness? Do you exhort them to delight in their femininity? Do you spend as much time with them as you do with your other friends, showing them how much you care for them? Do you *know* your siblings?

I am the oldest in a family of six, and all of my younger siblings (at this writing) are brothers, so I am far from an expert on sister-sister relationships. However, all of my closest friends have sisters, and having spent a great deal of time around each of them, as one looking from the outside in, I would love to encourage you to take advantage of the beautiful gift of sisterhood. In so many instances, I have longed for a sister to share my heart with, to confide in, and to grow towards godliness alongside. Do not take your sister for granted, and do not forsake her for girlfriends outside of your family. Thank the Lord for the gift you have in her, and cultivate that relationship.

Know Your Siblings

What are their likes, dislikes? What makes them laugh? What makes them upset? What is their passion? What are their pursuits?

This does not have to be delivered in question-form; just spend time with your siblings! Spend less time bickering with them and more time laughing with them and loving them and encouraging them! Less time tattling and more time redirecting them yourselves, lovingly and respectfully. Being the oldest, I used to loathe being told that I was the example, but now, I'm grateful for the opportunity the Lord has given me to impact the lives of my younger siblings.

The beauty in the responsibility we have towards our younger siblings does not have to be learned in a foreign country sharing a bunk-bed like a Marine; it can be learned through acts of service and love.

No one knows my brother Trey better than I do—the same can be said of him: No one knows me better than he does. I know what he's thinking before the words are out of his mouth, and he can look at something and see that I will love or hate it before I've seen it myself. This is not a testament to our amazing chemistry as much as it is a testament to the fact that we have spent so much time together. We did not always enjoy each other's company as we do now (although it's hard to remember a time when we didn't). But being home educated alongside him and moving to a foreign country with him was the beginning of a beautiful relationship.

Trey and Daddy are at a homeschool conference in Mississippi right now. I started my day off on the phone with Trey, talking for about an hour about subjects that ran the gamut from ministry to sociopaths to alien abductions. If you have a sibling anywhere near your age (there are three "whole" years between my brother and I, and we're still able to be close), and you cannot have an hour-long phone conversation with them without awkward silences—you're missing out!

What about Much Younger Siblings?

I am almost twenty years older than my youngest brother, eighteen years older than the one above him, seventeen years older than the one above him, and fourteen years older than the one after that. My relationship with Micah, Judah, Asher, and Elijah is different than my relationship with Trey in that we did not grow up together—I was well on my way to being a grown-up by the time Elijah came home in 2004. The age gap between us has given me even more opportunities to serve my youngest brothers than I had with Trey. For instance, I never got to serve Trey by changing his diaper because I was on the tail-end of potty-training myself when he came along.

Big sisters who have several younger siblings like I do have an amazing opportunity living at home to watch their siblings grow up into young adults. This gift does not come without sacrifice. It can be easy to look at young ladies in other families who don't have the burden of dirty diapers, wrangling, schooling, and disciplining, and idolize their relatively unhampered existence; however, if this is how you feel, you might be surprised by how many young women without the blessing of much younger siblings to nurture envy the opportunity you have.

One of my closest friends and I have a lot in common—we are both black young women, homeschool graduates, and attend the same family integrated church. We tend to love the same music, take interest in the same films, and adore the same classic literature. Something else we have in common is the number of "littles" in our families, and the fact that our youngest four siblings correspond in age.

Some of our outings are the regular outings you would expect an eighteen- and twenty-year-old to take—we go to the movies, hang out at the mall, and have sleepovers like any other girl you know. Other outings, however, are very unique to our family situation, like the time when my parents were out of town, and her mother and grandmother took all of us kids to the Houston rodeo.

We had a blast! And I realized something special: With the double stroller in front of me, an infant strapped into his baby carrier, and miles of walking, riding, and eating ahead of me—even when wails erupted—even when tempers flared—even when hyper-activity would have put someone else on edge—I was used to my brothers. I was used to diaper-changing, potty breaks, feeding schedules, and discipline issues that I was able to have an amazing day full of responsibility . . . *and* fun. And I so love my brothers that it is my delight to sacrifice a bit of freedom so that they can have an outstanding time. It makes my day more fun to see the smiles on their sweet faces

Having younger siblings is an amazing opportunity for character growth and growth in practical skills. I would not have had as many opportunities to learn selflessness, patience, tenderness, or consistency if it were not for my four youngest brothers. They have not only caused some aspects of child-rearing to come second-nature to me, but have also taught me a lot about myself and my own sin nature in the process.

If you have younger siblings, and you have never quite seen them as the blessing that the Lord calls them (Psalm 127), I challenge you to think of them in new terms. Think of them as little "sanctifiers" in your life—tools that the Lord can use to stretch you and grow you into the woman he has called you to be, not just in terms of how they can benefit you by training you to be super-mom, but how they are a gift from God—not just an inheritance for your parents—but a gift to you—with their smiles and laughter, with their wide-eyed wonderment at God's creation and their unconditional love for you, their big sister.

I have learned to spend quality time with my younger brothers in a lot of the same ways I have learned to give my time and attention to my teenage brother. Almost every day, we run outside to play "Spiderman," a game that includes me singing the *Spectacular Spiderman* theme song while chasing a five- and three-year-old Spidermen around the backyard and playset. They also love to read, so anytime we see a book we think they might like, we pick it up for our daily reading time together. I also try to invest in their home education, teaching three-year-old Asher full time and helping with his older brother Elijah's school if Mama has an appointment to make or an errand to run. I also love helping them with their memory verses and taking opportunities to bring up Scriptural truths with them.

Invest in your younger siblings! If you have brothers, encourage them to become godly young men. Don't be afraid to get your hands dirty or do silly

JOYFULLY AT HOME: CHAPTER FOUR

things to entertain them. Pretty soon, you will be having fun yourself. If you have younger sisters, invite them into your lives, Model biblical womanhood for them when you spend time with them. Don't treat them like pests or impositions; instead, treat them like people who are looking up to you. As an older sister, you have an incredible responsibility to invest in them. And, as daunting as it sounds, that responsibility can be so incredibly rewarding.

If you do not have much younger siblings who need your help, and you are afraid that you are missing out on valuable training in that area, don't lose heart! The Lord has given you a freedom to minister in ways that your peers with younger siblings may not have the opportunity to minister. Later on in this book, I hope to talk about some other ways that friends of mine who don't have younger siblings have been able to reap the blessings of helping out with younger children in other venues.

Whatever the ages of your siblings—whether they are twenty years older or twenty years younger—your years at home are a perfect time to invest in building strong relationships with them. This will go a long way in promoting harmony in your home, and giving you the base you need for truly being a blessing in other relationships you will form throughout your life.

For more excellent advice on this topic, I want to recommend *Making Brothers and Sisters Best Friends* by Sarah, Stephen, and Grace Mally.

Mothers, fathers, brothers, and sisters are such precious gifts, and there are so many ways that our attitudes and actions towards them can contribute to a joyful atmosphere in your home—something that I will discuss in the next chapter.

CHAPTER FIVE

Contributing to a Joyful Atmosphere

Atmosphere. I love that word. So very all-encompassing. And much nicer than saying, say, *circumstances*, or *conditions*, or *environment*.

Most teenage girls that I run across would cringe at the idea of living at home after graduation for an extended period of time. They would think about the horrible relationship they have with their parents, the fact that they find their siblings utterly annoying, and the fact that the only things they think of to do at home include stimulating activities like watching paint dry.

Being a good daughter to your mother and father and showing kindness to your siblings are both ways to contribute to a joyful atmosphere in your home, but the attitude goes much deeper than mere actions. True joy starts in your heart. The crux of understanding the message of *Joyfully at Home* is to understand the beauty of finding your joy in Christ. This sort of joy is not so much a Pollyanna, Sally Sunshine view of life as it is an understanding of what a joy-sucking battlefield the world we live in can be.

Joy-stealers come in all different shapes and sizes, but, most often, the lack of joy starts in our hearts.

I think we all come to that point at one time or another in our "stay-at-home" journey.

When we first decided to shift our focus, to turn our hearts towards home, we were enthusiastic and vibrant, purposeful and driven, meticulous and focused, bright-eyed and bushy-tailed. We had a grasp of the bigger picture: a vision for the home as a hub of ministry and discipleship, as a training ground for life ahead, as a place where we can bless those nearest and dearest to us, an, in turn, turn that blessing outward, towards others in our church and in our community.

But maybe you're a little like me. You always start a new journey with delight and determination. But then something derails your passion.

The home is a hub for ministry and discipleship. Perhaps you haven't found your niche yet. Ministry in and from the home is something that you're still getting used to. Turning your focus outward instead of inward is a difficult journey in the individualistic society we live in. You're used to focusing on your own plans, and now you're working as part of a team. It's difficult to adjust.

The home is a training ground for life ahead, which entails much humility as we are consistently taught, trained, guided, and redirected by Mom and Dad, as we're refined by the Lord, as our besetting sins are cast in the spotlight of every day life, not hidden from those who know us best; we are sanctified in a way we never were before. And that's difficult.

The home a place where we can bless those nearest and dearest to us. Even when we're tired of them; when they snap at us; when it's easier to be "slow in anger" to people outside of our immediate family; when we realize that it was more fun to hang out with our friends because they didn't know us quite as well as our siblings do, and couldn't see our glaring sin natures as well; when we look at other homes as outsiders and paint the inner-workings as the perfect, blissful family unit; or when we forget that, even if there was such a thing as the perfect family, as soon as we entered it, our sin natures would derail the perfection.

We can also be a blessing to those in our church and community. Hospitality. Service. Cooking. Cleaning. It may seem romantic when debutants on the 1950s TV shows don June Cleaver aprons and get to hacking, but perhaps cooking just isn't your forte, cleanliness and organizational skills don't come easily to you, and social climates make you antsy and nervous. You have just realized that, no, just because you decide to embrace the high calling of a keeper at home does not mean that your heart thrills at the sight of dirty dishes.

What about all of the questions? Are you tired of people asking again and again what in the world you're doing with your life? Are you sick of the accusations, the undue sympathy, and the constant barrage of questions coming your way?

If you're just coming home, and you still have that rosy, gung-ho perspective—you've never once looked up and said, "This is harder than it looks!"—then God bless you. My intent is not to discourage you. But if you are thinking about coming home, I am going to be honest with you: this home-girl stuff is going to get old at some point. Some mornings, you will wake up on the wrong side of the bed—you won't feel like serving joyfully at home—you will want to snuggle right back into your bed and put the pillow over your head.

What do you do on these days when laziness, or selfishness, or depression strikes?

Turn your focus outward and upward.

When we do anything with "me" as the primary focus, we are bound to become frustrated. When we realize that we didn't come home because it was easy or always fun, but because it's a place that is going to challenge and shape us into the women we've been called to be, we realize that sometimes contentment is a battle! But when we fight it with dogged humility, when we fight with Christ as our focus, when we battle with him as our strength, we—or rather, he—will be victorious.

I don't know about you, but when I'm losing the battle, usually, my focus is on myself, not on the Lord.

What makes living at home worthwhile again, you may be asking yourself? All of the opportunities listed above. And those are also the things that make living at home sometimes difficult. But are we here because it's easy?

I hope not. I hope you're living at home—or considering the prospect of coming home—for the same reasons I am: because you believe that it's the position where you can glorify the King of Kings; because it's where you believe he's called you to be; because you are fully invested in that calling. Because Proverbs 31:10-31 is the kind of woman you want to be, and the kind of blessing you want to be to those around you. If that's the case, realize something: Count the number of times in Proverbs that it's woman is thinking about herself more than she is about others. True joy and productivity doesn't come from being self-oriented. It comes from being Christ-focused and, as an extension of that, others-focused.

This does not mean you will never feel discouraged or discontent. But what it does mean is that, when you feel those things, you have a point of reference for doing away with those feelings: Your focus isn't on the ease of a passing moment, but on the reflection of your actions in eternity. Whatever our circumstances, when the King is our focus—

Well, that's really the center of our joy, isn't it?

So how do we come across this joy? A lot of it has to do with what we are feeding ourselves. Are we reading edifying material? Do we spend daily time in God's Word?

We also need to be careful about what comes *out*. How do we behave around our family members? Do we treat them with honor and respect (Ephesians 4:32)? Do we speak kind words to them (Proverbs 12:18)? Do we put their needs before our own (Philippians 2:3)?

So many of us leave our best behavior for those outside of our immediate families. We learn to put on a happy face and to control our actions. We save the fruit of the spirit for the people we truly want to impress (Galatians 5:16-27). If our joyful demeanor is a mask that we only put on when we leave the house, then it is a farce. A truly joyful young lady blesses her family the same way she seeks to bless others.

It can be difficult. It's easy to put a mask on for people outside of your home—it's not-so-easy to fight the battle for joy twenty-four seven. As we strive, it is so important to keep the lines of communication with our parents open. As adult women living at home, there is a fine balance to strike between competence and independence (something I will discuss in a later chapter). Here are a few lessons I have learned about creating harmony in family dynamics:

Give Your Parents Your Heart

Proverbs 23:26 is a beautiful verse: "My son, give me your heart, and let your eyes observe my ways." We are commanded in God's Word to honor and obey our parents (Ephesians 6:1), not because they're perfect, or because they know everything, but because our God is a God of order, and if the family unit is going to work smoothly and effectively for the kingdom, all of the little nuts and bolts need to be moving in the same direction. Our parents need to have our hearts, to know that we're fully invested in our God-given role, and that we're all working towards the same goal. Otherwise, we can forget living *effectively* at home—in fact, we may as well forget even trying to live peaceably with them! The first step to living in harmony at home is to trust your parents as the God-given authorities that they are—despite their faults—and to determine that you will live alongside them and learn everything that you can during this season in your life. Once that determination is made, I promise, you will see your home life in a different light.

Keep the Lines of Communication Open

I don't know about you, but my life is much easier when my parents offer me clear-cut directives and spell out their expectations of me. Blessedly for me, I have parents who do just that. Daughters, there is nothing better you can do to improve your home life than to learn to communicate with your parents in a sensible, understanding way. It cuts down on confusion and exasperation (Ephesians 6:1-4). We aren't robots; our parents don't stick a coin in our slot every morning and expect us to walk through our days on auto. We have to communicate. What do your parents expect from you on a day-to-day, week-to-week, month-to-month basis? Something as simple as, "Jasmine, when you do such-and-such a thing, I don't like it—stop" (in much kinder, more biblically grounded terms) gives me something to go on. Something like, "Jasmine, by the end of the week, I want this done" or "Jasmine, it would really help us out if, every day, you did these chores" sets clear boundaries. I don't make plans that infringe on the expectations my parents already have for me on a given day, for instance, and because we communicate about what exactly those expectations are, no one has to become frustrated if they aren't met.

When your parents give you a directive you don't understand or don't agree with, learn to ask polite, respectful follow-up questions, and to make a gentle, biblical appeal when necessary. I love to talk to my mom for hours on end; I keep her up late when Daddy and Trey go out of town (I bunk with my mom whenever they go out of town—yes *still*.) Daddy likes to tease me about it when he comes home by rounding up my things: "Party's over.") But, for those of you who aren't used to talking to your parents frankly and openly, listen to me: Your parents love you. They want to hear from you. And trust me, in most cases, they don't bite.)

When You're at an Impasse, Learn to Submit

This one's hard, but if you keep those lines of communications open, you are bound to hear some correction from your parents. If you've made a conscious choice to live under the authority of your parents after high school, then know this: As an adult daughter, you are going to have to learn how to submit your will to the will of your parents. When I was a younger teen, the very *word* submit made my skin crawl—I wanted to be my *own* woman! But I had to learn that the authorities God had placed in my life weren't a punishment, but a blessing; my family and I were a team, and we all played in different positions, and were shooting for the same goal. Sometimes, daughters, you have to "take one for the team," so to speak, swallowing your pride, and trying to see things from a different perspective: Every hill is not a hill to die on.

Submission is not unique to daughters. Our mothers operate in submission to our fathers. Both our fathers and mothers are to submit to a local church (Matthew 18). All of us are to act in submission to the state (Romans 13). And, ultimately, our submission is to God's Word.

Don't Spend Your Discontent Moments Daydreaming about Married Life

It happens to all of us. We become discontent and harried and look out over that pile of dirty dishes and sigh about the day when you'll be able to be supper on the table for the man of your dreams—when there's a guy in your life who needs you, not just to change his diaper or to feed him his applesauce. But, as I hope to discuss even more in the continuing chapters, sowing habits of discontentment has two negative results. First, it takes our sights off of the here and now, and sucks the industry and joy out of today's service. Second, it becomes a part of our character and demeanor that is sure to hinder us later in life. Remember, this is not the only "waiting" season you will ever have to endure Should the Lord bless us with husbands someday, we may wait for job transfers, moving opportunities, a biblically-functioning church, the blessing of children... in every season of waiting, our response should be to rely on Christ as the true source of our joy. We will talk more about that in the next section.

Don't Try to Find that Loophole

"My parents are too strict" or "my parents are too lax" or "my parents and I don't agree about this and that" are all excuses that I've heard. The fact of the matter is, our parents are fallible flesh and blood, as are we: our parents are going to be wrong. We are going to disagree with our parents. But when we have a godly mom and dad striving to lead us in the ways of the Lord, the last thing we should be doing is nitpicking. We should be submitting to them joyfully, acknowledging their errors, and perhaps making note of things not to do in our future lives, but still learning all we can from people who can teach us so much by sheer nature of having lived so much longer than we have; and, beyond that, for many of us, because of our mutual love for the Lord. He gave you the parents he did for a reason; instead of complain, obey them—you will find the reason.

If You Want to be Treated Like an Adult, Act Like One

How does one act like an adult? Not by false displays of bravado and independence, but by responsibility, accountability, trustworthiness, and discernment. If you find your mother telling you to do something five times, don't automatically rattle of, "I'm not a kid anymore, Mom!" Think, *Does she tell me to do that 12 times because I have a tendency to hesitate or forget when she just tells me one? Is that something I should work on?* If your dad says, "You know, when you act like that, it's not very attractive, sweetheart; I love to see you behaving a bit more graciously." Don't immediately snap, "This is just the way I am, Dad, take it or leave it!" Think, *Gracious. All right, that's a word I need to think about. Am I acting graciously—is my manner pleasing to the Lord and a delight to my parents right now, or is it abrasive? How can I work on that?* When you're given a new responsibility, don't complain; an adult takes on responsibility with competence and worthiness, not by whining. Rise to the occasion. When you do something wrong, take responsibility; don't blame it on anyone else. Fall on the sword, apologize, and make a note to do better next time. Show true repentance and growth; adults make mistakes, but they shouldn't respond in the same way children do—they should grow from them.

Set Measurable Goals

Make your time spent at home full of activity and growth. You need to be doing something productive throughout the week, and you need to have at least one long-term project going. Don't sit at home spinning your wheels; an idling daughter is not an actively learning daughter. Communicate with your parents about something you could be doing on a weekly basis that blesses the body of Christ; talk to your parents about something you can do long-term that will build character, perhaps even bring in some income. I find that busy hands are happy hands; an active mind is a mind at peace. If you set goals that don't include getting married in the next six months—goals we can actually accomplish—as you see progress, I guarantee, your whole attitude will be different; there's nothing like feeling capable and having a direction.

Whether you want to be a caterer, a novelist, or a lion tamer, the Christian home is a training ground for building character that will be foundational to whatever your life's aspirations happen to be. Even if you don't live with your parents, show them honor and deference, and when they make an effort to disciple you, submit to that teaching with gratitude. What an amazing thing to have parents who care enough for you and who take their God-given responsibility seriously enough to display that care through the imparting of God's Word. It's something we too often take for granted.

For daughters with less-than-perfect parents: Newsflash, they're all less than perfect; it's the nature of the Fall. However, if your parents are non-believers, you can still respectfully disagree with some aspects of their lifestyle while learning from them. My own parents have experienced that; they didn't have the privilege of growing up in a biblically-functioning family like I do, but they can still utter wise proverbs that their parents taught them, and can still draw lessons from the lives of those that are older and wiser than they.

If you have a doctrinal dispute with your parents, may I humbly suggest that you go before the Lord in prayer and steep yourself in his Word instead of entering into fruitless arguments with your family members? I know of Calvinist daughters with Arminian daddies, and Arminian daughters with Calvinist daddies. Though the lines of communication should always be open, learn when to stop talking and to let God finish the work in someone's heart, and do what he's called you to do and pray. That goes for any dispute; unless your parents are asking you to do something blatantly contrary to God's Word, submit joyfully.

Last, but certainly not least, remember what was said of the Proverbs 31 woman? "She opens her mouth with wisdom, and the teaching of kindness is on her tongue" (Proverbs 31:26). A very big chunk of creating a joyful atmosphere in our home starts with what the KJV calls, "the law of kindness" being on our tongues (Proverbs 31:26). James 3 speaks of the danger of the tongue, and that member's destructive influence can wreak havoc in our homes. Aside from setting our hearts on the things of the Lord, I would argue that controlling our tongues—even when those around us are not controlling theirs (Proverbs 15:1)—is half of the battle of contributing to a joyful atmosphere.

Growing pains are inevitable. I'm sure we can all attest to the truth of that statement. But, by God's grace, those tinges of growing pains can lead to the ripe fruit of righteousness.

Be joyful. Not because I said so, but because you know Him. Not because you want to look good to the outside world, but because you're living for him. Not because it's what you're "supposed to do," but because He gives you all the reason you need to live life abundantly. Not for any reason other than because it's what He's called you to.

And remember, as you strive to live joyfully at home, the key to serving in that sphere: Philippians 2:1-11. Live it.

As we move forward, striving to cultivate joyful, fruitful relationships in our homes, I want to turn our focus towards one of the main stealers of joy for a stay at home daughter: discontentment. The next section is devoted to overcoming discontented singleness, and embracing our years in our fathers' homes as an opportunity to grow in grace and to grow in joy as we depend on the Lord's perfect timing in every season.

Part Two

CHAPTER SIX

What is Joyful Contentment?

Part of staying joyful at home is learning to live *in the present* and to suck the joy and industry out of every day of our single years. I believe one of the biggest obstacles we will face as daughters remaining joyfully at home is learning to remain content during our single years under our fathers' roof.

I remember, not to long ago, I was sitting with a friend, talking about how she was spending her time these days. She was in her early twenties, would be graduating an online college program soon, and was using all of her time and energy to be a blessing to her family. Life had taken her on an interesting journey, from being at a prestigious state college with a full-ride scholarship to coming home to minister to her family. She was a bright, joyful young lady, enthusiastic about the things of the Lord, and diligent in seeking opportunities to serve others. Well meaning people who saw what a treasure she was had started raising their eyebrows and winking, "Oh we'll be praying for your husband—he's on his way."

"I hate it when they say that," she confided. "I don't want to be a girl who gets my hopes up about exactly when I'll be married. I don't want to be distracted that way; I just want to be content working hard where I am."

Her words and the attitude that they exemplified stuck with me. How many girls did I know with that kind of attitude towards their singleness? I could probably count them on one hand. On the other hand, I knew infinitely more young women who felt the exact opposite way about their current state.

"Oh, Lord! When, *when* will I be able to get married?"

We cry it out at different times. We might be crying it out when we're feeling discontent with the monotony of day-to-day life. "Oh, dear Lord! I'm so very anxious for the day when I'll be able to look out past the pile of soiled laundry, the stack of dirty dishes, and the mound of school work to behold— and have a home of my own, where things will be infinitely easier!"

We might cry out when we're feeling romantic. "Oh, dear Lord! I'm so very anxious for the day when I'll be perfectly loved by a flawless man who will always have my best interest at heart, who will never disappoint me, and who will never ask anything of me that I won't be willing to give."

We might cry out when we're feeling insecure. "Oh, dear Lord I am so very anxious for the day when I'll be perfectly loved by a man who will complete me, with whom I'll always feel perfectly adequate and confident, and who will never take me outside of my comfort zone."

We might cry out because we feel that singleness is a *less than* state. "Oh, Lord, I am so very anxious for the day when the purgatory of singleness will be over, and when you will usher me into the gloriously heavenly state of matrimony."

We cry out because we don't understand God's sovereignty. "Oh, dear Lord, I am so very anxious for the day when you'll finally give me what I want to make me happy. I'm not really concerned about living in whatever state brings you the most glory. I just want what I want as soon as possible."

We cry out because we don't understand the bigger picture. "Oh, dear Lord, I am so very anxious for the day when my own desires will be satisfied, because I really don't understand what marriage and singleness are for. I'm looking through the lens of my desires, and not through the lens of the bigger picture."

Sometimes we literally cry. Tears stream down our faces as we mourn the state that we have been relegated to, because everyone knows that single girls are castoffs, while the married women are the true prizes. Sometimes, we get angry. We blame the Lord for making us wait, we blame the men in our lives for not seeing us as the treasures we are, we blame our parents for not helping us look hard enough to find what we're searching for. Sometimes, we simply grow despondent. Our countenances are weary, our mood is depressed, and we shuffle through life half-heartedly, just waiting for something better to come along.

And as I reflect on the attitudes that many young women have towards matrimony, I begin to worry about whether or not some of us are setting ourselves up for bitterness and disappointment the longer we must wait for marriage, not trusting in God's timing so much as gritting our teeth and bearing the single years as they pass by in a lonely blur. Something we would never want to consider would be the prospect that these "single years" aren't just indefinite—they're perpetual. Some of us won't get married after all. What if that "lonely blur" happens to be the life that God has called us to? Will we still trust him?

If there was a sure-fire way to ensure that every young maiden serious about biblical womanhood and a Christ-honoring marriage would be married by the time she was twenty-one, not only would I be applying it vigorously in my own life, but I definitely would not be holding out: I'd write a blog post about it, send out mass e-mails . . . and goodness, I'd get myself a bull horn and find the highest hill in Texas!

But, to my knowledge, since the preparation, the "waiting," and the marriage itself are all part of sanctification, and, therefore, all geared towards God's glory and not my own desires...alas, there is no magic formula. And, when I'm not too busy navel-gazing to look up and see the bigger picture, I'm glad of it.

You see, my friend knew that. She understood how detrimental it would be for her to become sidetracked by dreams of romance when her primary calling in every area of life was to be focused on Jesus Christ and how she could best serve him in whichever sphere he deemed to place her. She understood the joy of finding her sufficiency in the King of Kings. And she knew that her single years were just as important to glorify the Lord as her married years would be.

We need to live in the present while planning for the future. When we stand before the Lord, we will be responsible for the way we used *all of our time*, not just our married years. We need to learn, right now, to find our contentment in the Lord. As daughters, as wives, as mothers, every aspect of our lives should be geared towards him. As single daughters in the home, our long-term focus should not be on that husband of ours that may come along; it should be on the Lord's Kingdom. All of our other longings, desires, aspirations, and actions should be filtered through this lens.

Yes, I know, sometimes it's easier said than done. And how would I know that?

My biggest credential for talking about the joys of finding our contentment in Christ is the fact that I'm a single young woman of marriageable age. I know just where you're coming from. I've had moments where I have faltered on the journey towards contentment. I've had moments where I didn't keep the desires of my heart in line with the guiding focus of my life: Seeking the glory of the Lord. The reason contentment is such a soapbox for me is because it hits me where I live. So, as we travel this journey together, I want to share a few lessons I've learned about the battle to stay joyfully content by talking about six key areas that keep us from finding the value in our single years:

- A false view of marriage

- A false view of husbands

- A false view of self

- A false view of singleness

- A false view of God's sovereignty

- A false view of the bigger picture

As we move forward, I want you to keep this question in mind:

What would you do if I told you that you would never be married?

Or if I told you that you would be single for the next ten years?

Now, I know my audience well enough to know that some of your knuckles are white right now, and your eyes are as big as saucers: *Never married? Perish the thought!* For the sake of full disclosure, I will say that very few things are as exciting to me as the prospect of being a link in the legacy of multigenerational faithfulness that my parents are striving to impart to my brothers and me by imparting it to my own children, and perhaps being able to impart it to my children's children. And, on a less multigenerational-minded level, I'm a hopeless romantic, too! But something I've been thinking about lately is that my dream of getting married, like all dreams in my life—should be held in open palms, not clenched fists. Whatever my state, I need to be able to honestly pray, "Thy will be done." And if his will is that I remain single, the last thing I want to do is to forge habits of discontentment so early on in my life! And even if his will is that I get married someday, I want to spend these single years in a joyous pursuit of *him*, not matrimony.

Is that true of you, too? I hope it is. And I hope as we continue to grow in grace, it can be more true of all of us. As we continue to seek the Lord, may we truly find the source of our joy in a full-hearted pursuit of him.

Remember that friend from the beginning of this chapter? In that single statement, she exemplified the sweet, trusting spirit that I crave as I continue on the road to becoming joyfully content with God's timing. Just a few months after she said these words, I found out that she had started courting another friend of mine, who was present when she spoke them to me.

Not too long after that, they were getting married.

At the penning of this chapter, the couple is expecting their firstborn.

As the dust has cleared from their whirlwind romance, my friend hasn't changed much. She is still the same joyfully content and productive young woman I met last year. Her surroundings have changed, to be sure, and she's serving the Lord in a different sphere, having traded the life of a stay-at-home daughter for the life of a stay-at-home mom, but every time I speak to her, she is telling me about the many projects she hopes to accomplish. Principally, this girl still loves the Lord with all of her heart, and he is her guiding focus.

It was a smooth transition from God-focused daughter to God-focused wife. May that be true of each and every one of us as we continue to grow in him, and as we welcome his plans for our lives . . . all in his perfect timing.

CHAPTER SEVEN

Overcoming a False View of Marriage

In Need of a Fairy Godmother

Someday, my prince will come—but, first, I need a fairy godmother. I'll be going about some monotonous chore that I've done a million times. Let's pick toilet scrubbing. I'll be scrubbing the toilet in my rags, bored out of my mind, singing, "So This is Love" in my lovely voice (or make "In My Own Little Corner"—Julie Andrews style, but with this amazing Aretha Franklin twist. Hey! It's *my* fantasy!), watching my pathetic expression (on the gorgeous version of the face that could have been) in the water below when I feel a tap on my shoulder. I'll turn to see her standing there: the fairy godmother come to change my life with a sweep of her magic wand! A mere twenty-four hours (and a few Rogers and Hammerstein songs) later, I'll be riding off into the sunset with my handsome (and incredibly smitten) prince. In that one gaze, I will be transformed from the boring toilet-scrubber I was twenty-four hours before to a radiant bride waving sweetly and innocently at my shocked stepsisters as I race off in that pretty white carriage towards my new life.

Of course, given the fact that the vast majority of us will not marry princes, and that I don't expect to be among the chosen few that do, eventually, the toilets in my castle (read: apartment) will need scrubbing—whether I'm living on an English countryside, in a cottage in France, or in a bustling city in Nigeria. And as I won't be able to do it in the resplendent dress I wore to the ball, I'll need to change into some of my old rags, get on my knees, and have at it. Oh, I'll be married, yes; but on the other side of the threshold that strong-armed Prince Charming (just plain old Johnny, in reality, my heart though he may hold) just lifted me over lies a home much like the one I've already been living in, and even more responsibilities than I left behind.

It's a theory that I've long held: I don't think most of us think about the "over-the-threshold" part—we get caught up in the carriage scene, where we're waving goodbye to our boring old life and stepping into the fantasy world. There's a reason why Disney movies stop at the wedding (and the cheesy sequels that come out ten years later don't count): to show us normal married life would ruin the illusion of perfection.

Have you ever heard the phrase, "The grass is always greener on the other side?"

Marriage *is* such a beautiful union (Ephesians 5:22ff), a state that many of us (I'd venture to say *most* of us), Lord willing, will someday occupy. I believe that marriage is something that the unmarried of us should be thinking about—we should be praying and seeking the Lord's will in finding and preparing for a spouse, leaning on our parents' guidance during this critical time of preparation, but, also realizing that our single years are fleeting, and that this unique time of ministry will not be around forever (1 Corinthians 7:34-35).

But, let's face it: When daughterhood gets tough, when the day-to-day toils become monotonous or difficult, when we don't want to apply and stretch ourselves, or when we're drowning in starry-eyed aspirations of romance, it can be easy to imagine a world where we are the queens of our own problem-free domains. In doing so, we start to view singleness as a less-than state.

Embracing a Fantasy of Marriage

Our idea of marriage starts to look something like this:

Johnny (Dan, Mike, Tom, Harry, Fabio, etc.) will come home from work to find you sitting on the couch reading to your adorable, well-behaved children. As he enters (handsome Irish—or Scottish, or Japanese, or Brazilian, or down-home all-American—devil that he is), you'll rise, and the children will scatter to their assigned corners of the room, cleaning up, setting the table, or just playing like the little cherubs they are. Johnny will sweep you up in his arms and gaze at you with the look that reads something like Elizabeth Barrett Browning's, How do I Love Thee. *And he'll kiss you and say, "You are always new, the last of your kisses was ever the sweetest." In the circle of his arms, in the living room of your beautiful home, after his long day at work at his amazing job, with his six-figure paycheck bulging in his back pocket, bills paid, pantry stocked, perfectly loved by a man in whose eyes you are flawlessly perfect . . . you heave a blissful sigh.*

Now, I realize that this scenario is over the top, even for someone with the most romantic sensibilities (and, as an aside, don't get be wrong: I love John Keats). But did you catch the problem in that fantasy? It was very *me* focused. And that's the key: Our ideals of marriage seem to focus all on *us*.

Something my mother has always taught me, though—a lesson I strive to embrace—is that marriage, like every other season in life, is a ministry opportunity. While I don't believe that a godly marriage should be devoid of that romantic love that we single girls tend to associate with it, that kind of love isn't the end of the story. Marriage is a stretching, sanctifying experience, and beyond the romantic facets of wooing, wining, and dining lie the day-to-day struggles from which unmarried young women are exempt. I want to talk about our false perception of Prince Charming in a later chapter, but right now, I want to mention that running our own homes isn't going to be any easier than the lives we have right now. In fact, some days, it's going to be infinitely more difficult.

"Well, all right," you may be thinking, "that's easy for you to say! You're single just like the rest of us—how should you know?"

It's true: I am single, and I am a single who is very desirous of that infinitely more difficult state. Sometimes, though, it helps me to get a foretaste of married life. That always brings me back to reality and out of dreamland.

How can one get a foretaste of married life, you might ask?

Well, you know when you have a pile of dishes in the sink, a load of laundry bleeping in the laundry room, a screaming baby in his playpen, two toddlers arguing over a toy in the living room, a list of chores as long as your arm, and errands to run before your mom and dad get back from their romantic weekend getaway... and you look to the heavens and sigh over the day when Prince Charming will come and rescue you from the depths of despair?

Hit pause. Rewind. And stop right before you prayed that Prince Charming would rescue you. . . and pray that the Lord would equip you to be a better helpmeet for Prince Charming by allowing you to conquer the difficult tasks before you. Because those very moments when we tend to wish in frustration that our prince and his noble steed would hurry up already are those moments where we are being stretched the most, growing in grace into the young women who will be able to take on much harder things on the other side of that threshold.

This was illustrated for me several months ago, when my entire family caught a nasty flu virus—and when I say my *entire* family, I mean everyone except for Baby Micah and me. While I do help out a lot at home, the full responsibility of taking care of my family rarely rests squarely on my shoulders. Although things can sometimes get hectic, with four adults and four younger children in the house, teamwork keeps us sane.

I didn't realize how much this arrangement spoiled me until everyone was down. Talk about a reality check! The Lord gave me a foretaste of what motherhood truly means (although I hope that the days I have to take care of six sick folks—four of them five and under—are scarce). I can imagine that Johnny (or Mike, or Dane, or Harry, or Julio) wouldn't look so charming doubled over and green in the gills. Diarrhea, vomiting, dizziness, runny noses, and coughing were the symptoms. When I didn't get sick, I stopped to think of what the Lord might be teaching me: 1) I need to add a really strong immune system to my resume; and 2) although it was my joy to take care of my family, and I praised God that I wasn't ill, I loved the reminder that running a home is *not* always easy and romantic. When my dad was well enough to join forces with me, I was *ecstatic.*

No, my experience didn't chase me away from wanting to be a wife and mother. But it did help me in my resolve not to imagine my married life as Snow White gaily and easily keeping house while woodland animals serenade me and help me turn down beds. And it helped me to be grateful for these years of singleness to develop the character I needed not to go crazy while my kinfolk were falling like flies!

Home-making is a ministry, not a fantasy. A realistic picture of marriage shouldn't put a damper on our prayers for the Lord to prepare our hearts for whatever the future might hold; rather, it should give us a true vision for what we should be praying and preparing for, and how we should view the season that we already occupy: Singleness is a ministry, too. Every season is an opportunity to glorify the Lord in the difficulties and in the triumphs.

When you ask for something that you *really* want and your parents say no, don't fantasize about a rich prince who will be able to supply all of your needs. Think, instead, of a hardworking man who sometimes will not be able to afford the latest and greatest appliance that you desire. When your parents take you aside to discuss a sin issue that has been cropping up in your character, don't fantasize about a doting prince who will never tell you anything you don't like. Think, instead, of a God-fearing man who is going to have frank conversations with his young bride when they reach a disagreement. When you do not want to do something your parents have asked you to do, don't fantasize about a giving prince who will never ask you to do anything you don't like. Think, instead, of a loving prophet, priest, provider, and protector to whom you will have to submit—even when (especially when) it becomes difficult (1 Peter 3:1-6).

When your little siblings get on your last nerve, don't think about perfect cherubs singing in perfect harmony in the next room. Think, instead, of your own sinful children who will need to be trained and redirected constantly (Proverbs 22:6). When your chores overwhelm you because you can't quite see the end of them, don't think about your perfectly-run castle with maids whistling in quiet corridors. Think, instead, of managing your own home, and the wealth of responsibilities that that entails (Proverbs 31:10-31).

When your romantic longings are more distracting than you think you can bear, turn towards the Lord, who satisfies all of our needs (Isaiah 58:11). Turn your passions down avenues that will glorify him, not those that would feed your flesh, and choose—daily—to walk in the spirit (Galatians 5:16ff), to be ruled not by your desires, but by the Word of God. And remember that though the romantic aspects of marriage are, indeed, sweet, as a cursory reading of Song of Solomon will tell us. . . they are not the end of the story.

What should we visualize when we look towards the future, then? If not the fairy-tale image pumped into our heads by a wealth of Disney movies or the breathless romance we have often envisioned, what?

Envision Ephesians 5:22-6:4:

> *Wives, submit to your own husbands, as to the Lord. For the husband is the head of the wife even as Christ is the head of the church, his body, and is himself its Savior. Now as the church submits to Christ, so also wives should submit in everything to their husbands.*
>
> *Husbands, love your wives, as Christ loved the church and gave himself up for her, that he might sanctify her, having cleansed her by the washing of water with the word, so that he might present the church to himself in splendor, without spot or*

wrinkle or any such thing, that she might be holy and without blemish. In the same way husbands should love their wives as their own bodies. He who loves his wife loves himself. For no one ever hated his own flesh, but nourishes and cherishes it, just as Christ does the church, because we are members of his body. "Therefore a man shall leave his father and mother and hold fast to his wife, and the two shall become one flesh." This mystery is profound, and I am saying that it refers to Christ and the church. However let each one of you love his wife as himself, and let the wife see that she respects her husband.

Children, obey your parents in the Lord, for this is right. "Honor your father and mother" (this is the first commandment with a promise), "that it may go well with you and that you may live long in the land." Fathers, do not provoke your children to anger, but bring them up in the discipline and instruction of the Lord.

Envision yourself in your fallen state, striving—by God's grace—to uphold the precepts in this passage. Envision your family and other Christian families you know as they sometimes falter along this journey, purposing to honor the Lord as husbands love and lead their wives, as wives respect and submit to their husbands, as they guide their children, who are to obey them as unto the Lord.

Envision life right now as what it is: A training ground for the dream you are holding so desperately in your heart. See your parents as disciplers who are, by God's grace, helping to mold you into the woman whose worth is "far above rubies" (Proverbs 31:10), that wife who is a "good thing" (Proverbs 18:22). See your household as a training ground that will teach you the homemaking skills that you will need to succeed (Titus 2:3-5). See your precious siblings in all of their sin nature, and realize that whatever work you help your parents do with them is training for the work you will do with your own little "cherubs" someday (Ephesians 6:1-4).

See life for all of its beauties and all of its hardships. . .

And put those dreams in their proper place.

Desire marriage in its proper context—as a vessel for God's glory—more and more, and you will grow to realize that it is nothing to sigh over. It is a battlefield to prepare for. We are God's children—we don't have to wait to fight the battle. We're fighting every day in singleness, for joy and wholeness in whatever state the Lord has placed us. Even, as we'll discuss in the next chapter, when we're fighting alongside imperfect husbands.

CHAPTER EIGHT

Overcoming a False View of Husbands

Enter: Prince Charming

When you were a little girl, maybe you were a bit like me, sitting in a circle of other young women, having been slightly brainwashed by the Disney fairy-tales you had seen, discussing Prince Charming in all his stunning glory. Our point of reference for true romance was, for the most part, handsome Disney princes with perfect hair, spotless breeches, and melodious tenor voices. I liked The Beast at first, and then I fell in love with Demetri from Fox's *Anastasia* (and, by extension, John Cusack).

When you are a teenager, perhaps that point of reference shifts from Snow White's nameless Prince to Elizabeth Bennett's haughty pursuer. Or maybe you prefer Captain Wentworth or Colonel Brandon. Perhaps you like Mr. Rochester or Heathcliff from the Bronte sisters' claims to fame, or Laurie, from *Little Women*, or Mr. Brook. When I was growing up, it was Moe from *The Road to Memphis*—I wanted Cassie to marry him *so badly*, and had ever since the first book *Roll of Thunder, Hear My Cry*—I am still waiting for Mildred

Taylor to pen a sequel where my dreams come true.

And then, perhaps, you realize that most of these heroes were all spun by the imagination of a nineteenth-century spinster, so you opt for a more spiritual approach and modify your standards. That was me again: "Fine, Lord, I want a man totally committed to your will in His life, passionate about the gospel and cultural reformation . . . who just happens to look just like Djimon Hounsou."

I'll do you one better: Once upon a time, I met an amazing young man. He was passionate about the things of God, and articulate about those passions. He was driven and unapologetic about living out his convictions, but he was compassionate and patient when he was teaching them to others. He knew how to stay focused, yet humorous during a debate, but also knew which things were really worth fighting for. He was empathetic, and he was an incredible listener. He was laugh out loud hilarious. He knew how to laugh at himself and the foibles of the world around him, with an unobtrusive, self-depreciating humor that was disarmingly charming. He was genuinely humble. And he was *so* good-looking. And, best of all, he loved *me*. So much that he asked me to marry him. "Come with me," this young man said, "to Israel, so we can minister to the Jewish refugees who have been displaced by World War II."

Oh, yes—did I mention that this young man was born in 1921? And the "I" I'm referring to is Harper, the heroine of the novel I wrote in first person several years ago. He's a little old for me because Harper was born in 1930. And he's a little too perfect because, although I might tell you that he was born the son of a pastor in New York City in the roaring twenties, in reality, he was born in my imagination at the beginning of the twenty-first century. My man is so perfect because... I made him up.

You think you've got it bad fantasizing about your favorite literary heroes or film characters? Falling in love with a figment of your own imagination is somehow more pathetic, don't you think? In my defense, though, you've got to admit, he *does* sound wonderful, doesn't he?

We all do it. Perhaps we don't write down the words we want to hear in our perfect proposals, but we've thought about them. And maybe we didn't jot down the height, eye color, hair color, and heritage of the gentleman who we hoped would come calling, but we wondered, idly sometimes, sometimes not-so-idly, who he could be. Perhaps your prototype isn't as fleshed out as the gentleman I just described (my excuse is that he was the main character of a story I first wrote back in 2002, and I'm sticking to it), but most of us would be lying if we didn't say that all of the fairy tales we've read and seen hadn't gone to our heads at one point or another.

Fantasy Husbands

The second major cause of discontentment is, I believe, a false view of husbands. When difficulty strikes, when boredom threatens, or when daydreams run rampant, some of us have a tendency to sing, "Someday my prince will come!" sometimes unconsciously building a pedestal for the man who will someday come and sweep us off of our feet. May the Lord help some of us if he never gets here, because we've wound all of our hopes into his perceived perfection.

For so many of us young women, our ideal man might look like [insert wildly attractive movie star's name here] on the outside, but, on the inside, his identity comes from making us happy. He is fine-tuned to meet all of our desires. He caters to our every romantic whim. He never disappoints us. He never aggravates us. He never falls short of our expectations, even though they hover somewhere in the stratosphere.

One young man once described him to me as the perfect man on the outside—and the quintessential woman on the inside. We want a girlfriend on the inside and a husband on the outside, a hunter-gatherer with Florence Nightingale tendencies.

When discontentment creeps up on us, instead of turnings towards the Lord for comfort, we turn towards the superhuman Prince Charming we've constructed in our minds, and he whispers sweet nothings in our ears (sometimes even with a fancy accent), and we're comforted by the idea that someday, our missing rib—our helper suitable—will walk into our lives and come alongside and complete us.

I didn't learn about my problem with fantasies until I paid close attention to the smirk that flitted across my mother's face whenever I talked about my pristine idea, and she asked (quite simply, as Mama always does)—"So have you ever met a man like that?"

I must confess, outside of the silver screen. . . I hadn't. I was basing my standards on a daydream.

Marriage to a Real Man

I have mentioned that several years ago, I began to work as my father's research assistant. I was inundated with marriage resources while he was writing *What He Must Be*. Beyond that, ever since I was younger, my mother would talk to me while I sat on her bathroom rug, all ears, and tell me the truth about marriage while she got dressed in the morning. I have watched my parents for years, my eyes growing keener as I've grown older. Through all of this research, through all of this watching, and through all of this conversation, although I am still convinced that marriage is a beautiful union, and still ever as hopeful of being married someday, I've realized something monumental: My husband will not be perfect.

I'm going to wake up one morning (not right away, perhaps, but eventually) and realize that we were made to be the suitable helpers of flawed men, and not the other way around (Genesis 2:19-25). Beyond that, we're flawed women who react to flawed men, sometimes, in very *flawed* ways. Some days, there will be trouble in paradise. And beyond *that*, we're not goddesses to be worshipped, but helpmeets who are going to be in the trenches. If we go into a marriage looking to have *our* needs met, we're eventually going to realize that marriage, like every other area of our lives, isn't all about us. In fact, in many ways, marriage is less about us than singleness is.

We should not develop the habit of placing all of our hopes in fallible human beings, because they are sure to disappoint us. Christ should always be the center of our joy (Deuteronomy 6:5), in singleness or in marriage. And, whether or not the Lord has marriage in our futures, that's a lesson we need to learn right now, because it's a lesson that will keep us focused on the Lord whether single or married. As single women, we need to learn to place our needs and desires at the foot of the cross, not on the alter of the perfect husband-to-be.

I am not a marriage counselor (given my years of experience as a wife and mother, I think that's probably a healthy position for me to forgo), but, as a single woman, I want to encourage you unmarried ladies to grasp this right now. Not only does it give us a more realistic perception of husbands, but it also helps us to relate better to the young men in our lives. We tend to stop sizing them up when we realize that our tendency is to make them innocent bystanders to our romantic whims and fancies, and we realize a revolutionary concept: They're only human. This understanding gives us a more realistic perception of what married life would be like, ("What?! He won't sweep me into his arms and recite Yeats every day after work?"), but it also helps us to engage in meaningful, pure relationships with the Christian young men we encounter, rather than eyeing them with romantic ulterior motives ("Oh, my soul! He said hello! He loves me. I wonder what size tux he wears...")

But what happens when our problem isn't just building a fantasy man, but sighing after a certain young man in particular? Here, I can speak from experience.

"But I Want *That* One!"

This struggle was summed up perfectly by a question I received not too long ago:

> *I'm struggling with my thoughts. There's this particular young man I know, that I would REALLY like to marry. And no matter how hard I try, I find myself thinking about him every day and ALL day long. How in the world do I get "free" from this? I mean, I don't want to pretend like he doesn't exist (ie: convince myself that he never was born), but at the same time, I know I shouldn't think about him ALL the time. Do you or others have any advice? And also, should I maybe not allow myself to want to marry him??? I'd appreciate any thoughts and advice.*

This is a hard question to receive. On the one hand, the answer is simple: "Just give it over to the Lord." On the other hand, however, "giving it over to the Lord" is not a one-time prayer, three magic words, or a switch you can turn on and off at will.

I remember sitting on a chair in my dad's office sobbing about a similar situation (which is a familiar setting for my anecdotes), and realizing that the Lord might be using my struggle to teach me something. Maybe when this certain young man came to my mind, I needed to pray for him. Maybe the Lord was showing me his admirable qualities so that I would file them away for traits in my future spouse. Maybe the Lord was teaching me a lesson about contentment. Perhaps I would someday end up marrying the man I was, frankly, pining over. In hindsight, the Lord has afforded me the wisdom to see that he knew what was right all along, and I'm very glad my daydream did not come true.

At the time, though, I definitely considered that the last scenario would be the best-case scenario. My mother later reminded me, however, that, whatever the outcome of my current struggle, I had been called to be faithful in this situation: to use my single years to glorify the Lord, to wait patiently until he revealed to me, not through wild imaginings, but through a solid sign of commitment, that the young man I was thinking about was the man he intended me to marry. I think one thing that kept me holding on to my struggle was the slim possibility that I'd get married to the man I was thinking about, and my struggle would be worthwhile. In reality, though, even if I married him six months from then, I'd been called to turn every distraction over to the Lord *right now;* I was to be wholly devoted to him right now (Isaiah 58:1-8), because his love is utterly, beautifully sufficient.

Did *that* make my feelings go away? No. I'm a passionate soul—my feelings linger quite stubbornly. And though I'm not convinced that we can control our feelings, I think that we can control our reaction to those feelings.

Take Those Feelings to the Lord

The first way is, of course, through taking those feelings to the Lord (2 Corinthians 10:5). We can close our eyes and grit our teeth and ball our fists all we want, but if we're not consistently on our knees before the Lord in prayer, our struggle is in vain. I didn't pray for the young man's future wife. I didn't pray for my future husband. I didn't pray that the young man would be my future husband (well, not often...). I prayed *Thy will be done.* In praying that prayer, in submitting my emotions and my hopes for the future to the Lord, I found a freedom that I never could achieve through my own self-help remedies. I didn't know where those feelings came from, and I didn't know their purpose, but I did know that I served a sovereign King who had something to teach me during that experience. I'm still learning, but He's a patient teacher.

Embrace Accountability

The second way to control our reaction is to embrace accountability. I talked to my dad about my feelings far too late. By that time, I had lost my appetite, I was mopey and withdrawn, and I had so many feelings pent up inside that when I opened my mouth to express them, all that came out were inelegant sobs. The thing about a lot of us girls is that our emotions affect every aspect of our personality. Try as we might, we can't compartmentalize our strong feelings. I've found that being open with both of my parents about what I'm feeling and for whom: 1) eliminates the stress of trying to keep an embarrassing secret; 2) turns that embarrassing secret into an opportunity to build a stronger relationship with my parents; 3) let's my parents know where I am emotionally, and helps them as they prepare me to become the wife of one of the men who drives me crazy; and 4) gives them a point of reference when they need to admonish me for the occasional moroseness brought on by my— shall we call it a crush? That seems so trite.

Trust Your Parents' Counsel

That leads me to the third way to control our reaction to our feelings, which is to trust your parents' counsel. If you are a young woman who has purposed to submit to the biblical counsel and accountability of your parents during the courtship and marriage process, now is a good time to practice. Be honest with your parents about your feelings for certain young men. Take to heart their admonitions about things you need to work on before you are ready to be married. Consider any praise or reservations that they may have about the young men in your life, especially those whom you are particularly interested in. Speak frankly with them about qualifications for your future spouse, and be open with them any time you think you may have met that young man. I don't know about you, but I'm not planning on entering into an arranged marriage. If I expect my parents' wise aid in choosing a spouse, I need to make sure they know where I am emotionally at all times. Their counsel and their involvement is, as I have said time and again, invaluable.

Watch Your Tongue

The fourth way that has helped me to control my reaction is to watch how I spoke about the situation. I have a horrible habit of pressing the instant replay button in my brain; I have a knack for remembering everything that's ever said to me, the facial expression of the person who said it, their tone of voice when they said it, and my theory for why they said it. It comes in handy when I'm writing a story, but it's a bear when dealing with emotions. If I wasn't careful, I hit rewind every time I was around girlfriends, playing the "he said, I said, what did that mean" game and digging myself a deeper hole. Our speech has such a huge impact on our thought life. We *must* be careful not to be silly and flippant when we're talking about something we're seriously struggling with; by the same token, we have to be careful not to be overly dramatic and passionate when we're talking about something we're struggling with. Don't rehearse your last meeting like a scene from a period drama, and don't psychoanalyze him like he's a mental patient. I'm not saying that mature conversations with girlfriends cannot be helpful, but we need to make sure that those conversations are *mature*. If we really want help, and not just an outlet for our giddy feelings, we need to refrain from immersing our friends in "he loves me, he loves me not" daisy-picking.

Remove Things that Irritate Your Symptoms

The fifth way to control our reaction to our feelings is to remove things that irritate our symptoms. Romantic literature? Check. Love songs? Check. Frivolous talk of future romance? Check. Movies wherein love is the central plot? Check. Even reading courtship stories? Oh, yes: check. You know what I found out? I missed those things more than I liked to admit. Because as miserable as my little obsession made me, I liked pinning my hopes on what I perceived as a dashing hero. I liked the flighty roller-coaster feeling; I even somewhat enjoyed the tinges of misery. And that let me know that I was casting myself in the roll of a romantic heroine instead of seeing myself as what

I really was: A young lady who needed help in focusing her heart's affections on God's will for her life, not on her own romantic inclinations. It was a hard pill to swallow, and even though sometimes, I still feel the lump in my throat, acknowledging my downfall in that area really helped.

Learn to Wait and See

The sixth way that helped me was to wait and see. We don't know what the Lord's plans for our lives are. Someday we might pray vehemently for feelings to be removed that were meant to be there, and we'll continue to struggle with them until the object of our emotions marries us already (did I just say that out loud?). Someday, we'll pray vehemently for feelings to be removed and we'll wake up one morning to find that they have been. In any case, we have to wait patiently, and to strive to be faithful while we wait, to trust the Lord's sovereign timing, and his plan for our lives. There are seasons where we must struggle. We mustn't despair during those seasons. We must search out the lesson the Lord is trying to teach us.

Allowing Him To Lead

The seventh way that can help us to do away with crushes is to understand how important it is for us to allow the men in our lives to lead. In the midst of the desperation that being interested in a specific young man can cause, we often throw our sense of discretion out the window. We might try to think of ways to catch his attention, or to declare our affections.

What's so wrong with taking the lead?

Marry Kassian writes in her book, *Girls Gone Wise in a World Gone Wild*, in light of the nature of women and their complementary difference from the men in their lives (which I will discuss in more depth in the following chapters):

> *So here's my advice to you—unmarried or married—who want to be Girls-Gone-Wise: Let him drive. Wait for him to pick up the keys (physically and metaphorically). Hold back. Don't rush in. Give him a chance to initiate. Welcome his leadership. I know that nowadays, men are plagued with the sin of passivity. This is primarily due to their sin natures, but also in part because women have shoved them out of the driver's seat and brashly taken the wheel. I know that many women ache for their men to step up and be men. What I advise all the [young women] crying on my shoulder is this: "Reclaiming*

your womanhood is the best way to help a man reclaim his
manhood." We live in a world broken by sin. So this isn't easy.
But a Girl-Gone-Wise inclines her heart to embrace her role as
a woman and follow God's design.[10]

Yes, even if you *really* like him. Even if he doesn't seem to know that you exist. Even if everything in you is *screaming* out to make your presence known to him. . . the best thing you can do as a young woman to encourage godly manhood in the young men around you is to allow them to initiate. This does not mean that you avoid him like the plague (your lack of attention is almost as noticeable as being over-attentive—I remember once, I was so enamored with a young man that every time he came around, I would dive into the ladies' room or hide behind my dad or look off in the other direction when he came walking up to talk to me. It seemed completely logical at the time, and, of course now, every time I think about the wounded look on the poor man's face, I'd like to sink into the floor), but it does mean that you don't take opportunities to treat him with any more deference than you would any other man.

Do not, for instance, call him on his cell phone and ask to speak to his sister after holding him on the phone for thirty minutes. Don't litter his Facebook wall with one thousand and one comments about the goings on in his life when you are hardly even ever on Facebook. Don't gravitate away from groups to spend one-on-one time with him. Avoid coy flirtation as well. This could include things like batting your eyelashes or putting a certain swing in your gait when you walk away from him, touching him excessively while you're talking to him, on his shoulder, on his arm, or on his hand, or standing uncomfortably close when you talk to him.

Show restraint in your behavior towards this young man. When you think to initiate an action towards him, evaluate your motives: "Am I trying to get him to notice me by doing this?" "Would I be looking at him like that if I wasn't interested in him?" "Are my actions towards him God-honoring and edifying, or am I only trying to feed my flesh." Only you can answer these questions. Answer them honestly. Denial is not your friend.

Knowing that Desire Will Always Be Present

Believe it or not, our desire for certain things in life will not be wholly satiated once we're married. Some of us may wait anxiously for the children the Lord will bless us with. Some of us will then wait anxiously for the milestones in that child's life. We might wait for a financial issue to be resolved, or we may wait for a certain ministry opportunity to open up. The opportunities for waiting—for longing—will continue until the day we die. We need to find our sufficiency in Christ during these longing seasons, to dwell on him, to seek his heart. When Hannah longed for a son, she had no way of knowing how the Lord was going to answer her longing, yet she trusted him, even as she cried out to the Lord (1 Samuel 1).

You know what I like to think about even more than being a blushing bride, looking down the aisle at the man I've waited for, knowing by then his side of the story (although that sounds heavenly as well)? I like to think about having been married for fifty plus years, having been loved purely and freely by my best friend for the balance of my days, having sought hard after the things of the Lord together, having faced life's trials and triumphs side-by-side... I think I'll look at him one day while he's doing a task I've watched him do a million times, and I won't think of the wait so much as I'll think of the fullness of our time spent together. And I think what I'll feel and what I'll know then will be worth all of the wondering I may have experienced before he came on the scene.

Putting Romance in Its Place

Should I marry, I fully expect to be as gooey and romantic at times as I wouldn't want to be caught dead being in my single state. Beneath the goop, though (ah, that glorious goop), I hope there lies a true understanding that the all-encompassing goal of that union between two sinners is God's glory, and that it's only by his grace that the two who will become one can work towards a unified goal that will honor him (Ephesians 5:22ff). If nothing else, Prince Charming will not make my sin nature disappear. Even if he could be perfect, I could never be. We will still undergo sanctification on the other side of the glorious wedding day we catch ourselves fantasizing about, and I'm told that my husband will aid it in ways that I never imagined as a carefree single gal. To lighten the mood, though, I must add that I'm told that marriage will hold joys that I never could fathom as a single gal as well.

I am not waiting for a husband to come into my life and give it worth, nor can I give any man's life true worth. I am seeking my worth in Christ, in the state I'm already blessed to occupy. Whether I have—or ever have—a husband or not, the Lord should be the center of my joy, and the focus of my pursuits. That will make me a better wife someday should the Lord call me to wifehood, yes. But beyond that, it will make me a better ambassador of Christ here on earth regardless of my state. As we'll discuss in the next chapter, this starts with living every moment in pursuit of true spiritual growth... starting with the single ones.

CHAPTER NINE

Overcoming a
False View of Self

Strong and Silent vs. Chatty Cathy

My favorite president is Calvin Coolidge. Aside from his approach to politics, I love how his personality is often described: "Silent Cal" was a man of few words, wise and reflective, calm and calculating. I love the story his wife Grace often told of a young woman who sat next to President Coolidge at a dinner party and remarked that she'd just bet that she could get him to say three words before the evening was out. Without glancing in her direction, the president coolly responded, "You lose." Mm hm. Silent Cal was my kind of man. And Grace Anna was my kind of woman. Charming, vivacious, and outgoing, she was the perfect balance to her introverted husband. As a natural extrovert, I always plotted on marrying a reserved man, with still waters that ran deep, with depths that few people got to plunge. Dry humored. Quick witted. Decisive.

Until I got a little older and got to know enough young men to realize that some of the quietest guys I knew were the most arrogant. They weren't quiet because they understood the merits of Proverbs 10:19. They were quiet because they felt that whatever company they endured was graced by the sheer nature of their powerful presence. They were distant, not because of shyness and humility, but because of pride that kept them from wanting to talk to peons (a.k.a., we regular folk).

All right then. I decided I would marry someone talkative and gregarious. Warm. Accessible. Jovial. A real people person, the type of guy that never met a stranger. In fact, I couldn't believe I ever wanted to marry an aloof man. I hated those guys! But then, those buoyant, talkative types—couldn't *they* get old, too, what with sticking their feet in their mouths sometimes, or talking through the moments that ought to be silent? Perhaps not being taken as seriously? Poor, conflicted me. Poor young men, whose personality types had been shoved into two narrow boxes. I now find it comical to imagine that my future husband (a Silent Cal, perhaps) is crying out to the Lord, "Please don't send me a drama queen, God! Anything but that!"

Maybe the Lord is going to put dramatic me in his life to teach him some lessons and to balance him out, and I think, whatever personality my husband has, he will do the same for me.

Praying for Our Husbands the Right Way

Oftentimes, when I hear young women speaking about what types of men they would like to marry, they don't talk about the type of personalities that would challenge and grow them... they talk about the type of personalities that they would fancy. Much like myself, when I was debating over whether I wanted to marry Silent Cal or Chatty Cathy, their view about marriage wasn't towards sanctification or growth at all. It was focused on what *I* would like, what would balance *me*, what would make *me* comfortable, what I wouldn't need to change for.

For instance, I always prayed for a man who could tolerate the fact that I am extremely emotional. But I never considered mortifying the sin that was a lack of self-control on my part. I prayed for someone whose laid back personality balanced out my perfectionism. I never thought to mortify the sin of pride in my life. I prayed for a decisive man because I grow impatient with visionaries who are juggling fifteen ideas at once. I never once thought to pray for patience or a submissiveness that would teach me to ride the roller coaster of being married to a visionary man.

And so on and so forth.

I believe that, many times, we young women become discontent in singleness because we get tired of our sin natures. We chalk up every frustration we have in our lives now, and imagine that marriage will reverse that frustration. This is somewhat linked to our false view of husbands, yes, but I believe it goes much deeper than that: We have a false view of ourselves. We tend to view marriage and men as something we can throw together on an assembly line. I'm *this* way, so he'll be *that* way, I like this, so he'll do that, I don't like this about my life, so when I'm married, life will be this way. . . And if we can get the perfect combination, the sins we struggle with in singleness will vanish in the light of love, compatibility, and planning. Because everyone knows that the sins we struggle with now aren't *our* faults; they're caused by our surroundings. A change of pace would eradicate them completely, yes?

In doing so, we miss the big picture: Marriage entails *sanctification*, as we've said. Which means that while, in a sense, your husband might be the corresponding half that will make you whole (to wax a bit poetic), we can't expect the pieces to fit together perfectly, because we're flawed human beings who, in every season of our lives, will experience trials that will drive us to the cross. If our marriage could remedy every sin and discontent in our lives, we wouldn't need the gospel. Marriage does not bring automatic righteousness. We will not suddenly wake up one morning manifesting the fruit of the spirit just because we've said our wedding vows. Growth and character are things that we can pursue right now, in singleness, and things that we should be pursuing. And pursuing them will keep us so very busy that we will have little time to pine over Prince Charming knocking on our doors. In fact, pursuing them will make us much more capable and realistic wives if Prince Charming should come around.

Again, how do I know all of this anyhow?

Unfortunately (but realistically) I'm not perfect. I didn't just wake up one morning with twenty years of marriage experience behind me, ready to tell all you single girls the secrets I've learned. My mother taught me this, and I'm sure, for many of you, your mom has been teaching you the same lessons. I can see it with my own eyes, as I'm sure, for many of you, if you will take off your romantic blinders, you will see these lessons being played out right in front of you. Pick up a book like *Sacred Marriage* or *What did You Expect?: Redeeming Realities of Marriage* to hear Gary Thomas and Paul Tripp expounding upon these principles to a wedded audience... and take heed to learn these lessons in singleness, to save yourself—and your husband—a rude awakening later on.

A false view of marriage also causes us to view single men like they are items on a grocery shelf. We want to check their ingredients, compare prices, and take stock of their health value the same way we would a can of soup. Again, this causes us to view them, not as brothers in Christ, but as candidates for matrimony.

Treating Our Brothers in Christ Like Brothers

I was trying to be charming.

There was a group of teenagers gathered around talking about something I can't quite remember now. What I do remember was that I was fourteen, and that I was nervous. And then one of the coolest guys I knew turned towards me and flashed a smile that made me even *more* uncomfortable. And so I did the inevitable, ridiculous thing that insecure teenage girls are supposed to do in situations like those: I turned to walk coolly away from the conversation... and I ran into a wall.

Yes.

In front of the coolest guy I knew ... I ran into a wall.

What made it worse was that he immediately rushed over, eyes wide: "Are you okay?"

I was not okay. I felt the beginnings of a splitting headache. But it was nothing compared to the humiliation that I knew would linger long after I left the company of my peers. *I ran into a wall!*

That young man is now happily married, and my humiliation has dissipated; the embarrassing tale has become (as many similar tales in my life become) a perfect illustration of something that is a struggle for many of us.

Finding the Cure

Unfortunately (probably fortunately, actually), God's Word doesn't give a carefully outlined list of do's and don't's for friendships with our brothers in Christ (although it does speak to this issue, as we will discuss a bit later), and so I'm hesitant to give a list of do's and don't's of my own invention. Really, our heart's attitude is the most important factor to consider here. We can seem pristine in our actions towards young men in our lives, and our thought lives might still be displeasing to the Lord. But I feel your pain; life seemed much simpler when we were younger, didn't it?

Boys had cooties.

End of story.

Of course, as you grow older, you start to realize that, not only do boys *not* have cooties... but those qualities that used to repel you when you were five either began to dissipate (I don't know many sixteen-year-old guys who still roll in the mud unless there's a contact sport involved), or, instead of repelling, begin attracting (when did teasing sneers turn into appealing grins?!). Our age of the awareness that boys actually aren't all that bad tends to vary from female to female. But, quite inevitably, it happens.

This is often a difficult subject to tackle. If we spend too much time over-analyzing our actions towards them, and their actions towards us, we're liable to become basket-cases around the young men in our lives. We'll find that we're more and more awkward around them, and that awkwardness might cause us to miss out on some fruitful friendships. My advice is usually to "be yourself." But if you're anything like I've had a history of being, when you're around certain young men, you tend to forget who "yourself" is. Simple tasks like walking across a room or clearing your throat to say "hello" become monumental accomplishments.

There is a simple answer to our problem:

Don't talk to boys. In fact, don't even look them in the eye.

When you see them coming, walk in the other direction; if there's nowhere to run, duck into the women's room; if there's no women's room nearby, dive behind a trash can. When you're forced to talk to them, act completely unnatural. Avert your eyes, look for the exit, giggle, and stammer. Yes, stammer a lot.

Then you'll never have to worry about getting to know them, and if you never befriend them, you'll never struggle with crushes. That's the key.

I'm being facetious, of course!

But, often, growing up, that was the only way I thought I could avoid "inevitable" crushes. *Hide.* Of course, later, I realized that to think that it was impossible to guard my heart revealed that I had bought into a false definition of the heart I was trying to guard, or the emotions that I was trying to keep at bay. And I had a false perception of *myself.* I was viewing myself as an incredibly eligible young woman who was forever in danger of forming an attachment to an incredibly eligible young man. But more on that misconception a little later in the chapter.

Guarding our Hearts

Remember what this chapter is all about: having a false view of ourselves when it comes to our romantic aspirations. This false view manifests itself in many ways; one way is a false view of our hearts. If we don't have a proper understanding of our hearts, then we can forget trying to guard them, because autonomous emotions cannot be harnessed. So, first and foremost, if we want to guard our hearts, we need to understand that, if God's Word commands us to guard them, they are, indeed, guardable.

> *Keep your heart with all vigilance, for from it flow the springs of life. Put away from you crooked speech, and put devious talk far from you. Let your eyes look directly forward, and your gaze be straight before you. Ponder the path of your feet; then all your ways will be sure. Do not swerve to the right or to the left; turn your foot away from evil. —Proverbs 4:23-27*

That sounds easy enough, right? It's *my* heart; *I'm* in charge here. If *I* have enough willpower, *I* won't ever fall into the trap of placing my heart's affections where they don't belong.

However, we are incapable of truly guarding our heart's affections unless they're centered right where our eyes should be focused; and we know that the safest place for our hearts' affections is in the hands of the Almighty. It is so easy to get distracted, and to take our eyes off of him and his purposes for our lives *today*, rather than trusting that he has tomorrow well in hand.

So how do we make sure our focus is in the right place? What are we feeding our hearts? What delights and consumes us? If we fill ourselves to the brim with romantic thoughts and inclinations, if all we can think about is courtships, weddings, honeymoons, starting a family, about how we could be married in as little as *six months* if the right guy came along tomorrow . . . then whenever we feel the pressure of those pesky heart palpitations, what's going to come out is a wistful sigh, not a reasonable jolt back into reality. If we're filling ourselves with God's Word, "with whatever is true, whatever is honorable, whatever is just, whatever is pure, whatever is lovely, whatever is commendable..." (Phillippians 4:8), then we'll be more on guard against such foolishness.

This is not a ban on Cole Porter love songs, Jane Austen romances, Disney princess movies, or even a healthy excitement and preparation for marriage, but it is a caution: We need to know when enough is enough, and to use discernment when we know we've gone overboard. If all you and your friends can seem to talk about when you get together is the solo you'd like your cousin to sing at your wedding, the cutest wedding dress you saw in a bridal magazine, or the way you plan to wear your hair to best flatter the veil you chose, and you're not actually engaged—you've gone too far.

When our affections are centered on the Lord, how are we treating others? We are to *love* one another (John 13:34-35, Romans 12:10,

Ephesians 4:1-3). How are we to love the young men in our lives? God's Word tell us that we're to treat them like brothers, with all purity (1 Timothy 5:1-2). This should not only lead us to control our actions towards our brothers, from the type of clothing we wear, to awkward or flirtatious behavior that might confuse them or cause them to stumble, but it should also lead us to control our thoughts about a young man that is not, and most likely never shall be, our husband. Allow your brothers in Christ to be gentlemen without having to worry that their every conversation will come off as a hint of eternal affection, or their every smile, glance, or act of deference will be taken as a token of undying love.

Also, even after you leave the presence of young men, watch how you talk about them to your girlfriends. I'm sure these unwitting young men would not appreciate our giving him a reputation among his female peers, especially not from our biased representations of his actions. A good tip is not to say anything about a young man to your girlfriends that you wouldn't want him to overhear. Trust me, the less you talk about young men like marriage prospects, the less inclined you'll be to behave awkwardly around them. Believe me, I know from experience (a friend of a friend of a friend's cousin told me once. . . .)

Remember from the last chapter: The goal of talking about these things is accountability, not giddiness.

Do not underestimate the importance of emotional purity. It can seem harmless to let our emotions run wild, but, not only is it an unhealthy way to view young men in your life, but it also diverts your focus from the King of Kings. Crushes seem to occupy *most* of your thought time. . . . and we know that only the Lord should hold that place. It helps to remember that the Lord has a bigger plan for our lives than marriage and children, and that plan is to glorify him with whatever gifts and talents he has given us, in whatever season of our lives he's placed us. When we get distracted from what he's called us to do in this particular season in our lives, we are hindered from serving him as we should in the here and now.

Do we really need to wring our hands, to wait in wonder, to doubt and maneuver in order to understand God's plans for our lives? In those difficult times, whether there's a certain young man who keeps diverting our attention, the fact that our single years seem to stretch a long way behind and a long way ahead of us, or whether we're not even sure that marriage is the Lord's plans for our lives, we can trust that he has things well in hand (Romans 8:28).

How Eligible Am I?

This goes back to what I was saying earlier in the chapter about a false view of ourselves and our eligibility. As my mother has always told me there's no reason to be anxious about marriage; I'm not as eligible as I think: There's only one man for whom I was intended to be a "helper suitable," and thank goodness it's not up to me to figure out who that is! When the time comes, the Lord will move things into place in the beautiful way that only he can orchestrate things, and there will be no need for doubts or guessing games.

Instead of pinning all of our hopes on marriage "fixing" us, we single girls would do well to wrestle with our sins in the here and now, building character that will benefit us should we remain single or should we marry. I am not suggesting that there isn't a level of compatibility that needs to be in place before two people decide on marriage (if he doesn't laugh at my jokes, we can't be an item—that's just that), but those wiser than we are can help us to navigate the difficult waters of expecting marriage to hide our sin natures and really, truly seeking the Lord's will in finding the man to whom you are best suited to be a helper suitable.

I don't now if I will marry the strong, silent type, or the jovial, outgoing type. I don't know if he'll be a visionary who is always spinning in ten different directions at once, or the type of man who has the same, steady vocation until he dies. I have no idea if I'll marry at all. But here's what I do know from God's Word: If I marry a man who loves the Lord, and who loves me, as I endeavor to love him in the sense that the Lord has called me to, I will grow in ways that are currently unfathomable. If I commit myself—right now, today—to submitting every area of my life to Christ, and to prayerfully trusting in his will as he allows me to grow in grace, it will make me better able to do so once I am married, or a better ambassador for him as I remain single.

That sounds like a win-win to me. Instead of waiting for marriage to straighten us out, let's endeavor to seek the Lord's will now as he grows and matures us, by his grace. Single or married, it's something we all need to do! The gospel is the only "cure-all" there is—I'm so grateful we serve a sovereign King who will bring the work to completion (Philippians 1:6). I want to be a gospel-focused single because I know that marriage is not the only state in which the Lord can use me, a concept we will discuss more in the next chapter.

CHAPTER TEN

Overcoming a False View of Singleness

A Waste of Potential

I was talking to an older woman several weeks ago, and she asked if any young men had come to my dad to ask for my hand in marriage. When I answered (I hedged, as I always do when asked that particular question. As an aside, I fantasize about announcing any relationship I might have by going to church and seeing who notices the engagement ring—about many things I am very open: my own relationship status is not on the list. So I could be courting right now and not writing about it. I'm not, of course. But then again, I could just be saying that to throw you off my trail. . . .), she replied, "I can't wait for the right man to come along and sweep you off your feet. It'll be so fun to watch!"

Because I don't like the idea that onlookers will watch my love story unfold as if it's a Jane Austen film, because I was in the process of writing a series about contentment and thought her reaction would make a good illustration, and because I am secretly as devious in my core as the taunting, contrary six-year-old version of myself, I said, "That would be nice—but, you know, I might not end up getting married. Perhaps the Lord will call me to a life of singleness."

To which she responded. "Excuse me for saying it but . . . you not being married would be such a *waste!*"

She meant it as a compliment, of course, and I took it as such. In my quest for contentment, I don't want to become an anti-marriage warlord ("Are you implying that I need a *man* to make me happy?! I am *SO* content! Don't I look content??") She sweetly went on to state her opinion of what a great wife I would be. But I did get to thinking about her words—hadn't I better get married as soon as possible if singleness was a waste of my God-given talents?

A Context, Not a Condition

The other day, when I was talking to my dad about this particular chapter, he said something that resonated with me: Singleness is a *context*, not a condition. It isn't a punishment. It isn't a "less-than" state. It isn't second-class. It isn't superior to marriage. It is just a context for women to serve the Lord, while marriage is a different context. The women in both states are equally valuable in God's plan, or he wouldn't have placed them there. Whether single or married, we're in that state because it's where we can best glorify the Lord. The moment his plan for us involves marriage, rest assured, he will provide a spouse. I don't believe that the age at which you get married necessarily reflects your level of godliness and maturity. I don't believe that a life of singleness is a curse or a punishment. And when I hear young women say things that betray just the opposite, my heart breaks for them.

As an aside, there is a difference between flouting and delaying marriage and contentedly seeking the Lord's will while single. This chapter is addressed to young women who *desire* marriage, but have not met the right guy just yet.

I believe that marriage is something to be sought after, and I believe that young people should be serious about preparing for matrimony. I think the "ministry of marriage" (a term my father talks about in *What He Must Be)* is too often overlooked, especially by young women who have been fed the lie that life ends when you get married, and that holding on to the freedom and independence of singleness is more important than desiring to be the link in the godly legacy that our parents have imparted to us by imparting that legacy to our children and our children's children.

In *What He Must Be* in the chapter "The Ministry of Marriage", my father writes:

Young men and women seeking advice on how they can serve the Lord often pepper me with questions. Some sense a call to ministry; others simply desire to play their part in the Great Commission. Still others are merely longing to find deeper meaning and purpose. They expect me to extol the virtues of seminary, education, missions, or summer internships. Perhaps they are looking for a word about impacting the marketplace or traveling overseas to invest in the lives of the poor, needy, and lost.

However, they never expect the answer that I inevitably give when faced with such inquiries: "If you are serious about serving the Lord, get married (Proverbs 18:22; 19:14), pray that he gives you a house full of children (Psalm 127; 128), and bring them up in 'the discipline and instruction of the Lord' (Ephesians 6:4)." [11]

The ministry of marriage is not one to be forsaken. However, the season of singleness is not one that needs to be undermined.

I do believe that some people are given the gift of singleness (Matthew 19:12), but I don't believe that the "gift of singleness" should be an excuse for putting of marriage, selfishly pursuing our dreams without using God's Word as a measuring stick (1 Corinthians 7:34-35), opting out of marriage because we don't properly value the home (Titus 2:3-5), or using the gift of singleness as an excuse for an issue with submission (Ephesians 5:22ff).

Gratefully Single

Yet, as much as I value marriage, I can truthfully say that I am gratefully single. Because, as Daddy says, this is a context, not a condition. Singleness is not purgatory to marriage's paradise. Every season of our lives has been granted us as an opportunity to serve the Lord. If we miss that truth, we will fritter away our single years pining after marriage without ever taking full advantage of the opportunities we have *right now* to serve him and to serve others in the very sphere we're so very desirous of: the home. We'll begin despising the very thing that could best prepare us for matrimony!

And while I never want to encourage young women to develop character traits just to "rope a husband," rather than focusing on how their character can please the Lord, here's something that I've learned from the godly young men in my life: one of the most attractive (and rare) qualities they'll find in a Christian young woman is that she is joyfully, industriously serving the Lord in singleness, not eyeing every young man that crosses her path as a prospective Romeo that will take her out of her gilded cage.

I love the Lord with all of my heart, and I don't have to wait for marriage to exert every bit of energy I have into becoming a woman after his own heart. The very gifts that young women talk about blessing their future husbands with could be used right now to bless their homes: They could be industrious (Proverbs 31:17), entrepreneurial (Proverbs 31:16), conscientious (Proverbs 31:21), wise and gracious (Proverbs 31:26), among so many other things, instead of thumb-twiddling or pining.

How are some of the ways that we communicate to ourselves and to others that single girls are not as important in God's economy as married ones?

Married > Single

"Oh, Kate is getting married at eighteen—she must be incredibly godly!"

My father was married at the tender age of twenty; my mother was twenty-three. He was married young because that was God's plan for him. The Lord meant for marriage to sanctify him, to gird him during his ministry, and to teach him lessons that would stabilize this young pastor as he began to preach. The Lord meant for my mother to be married three years later than my father because when she was twenty, he was only seventeen, and would not come to know the Lord until he was almost nineteen.

Mama had no way of knowing this. Had many of us been in her situation, as young as twenty-three, we would have been looking around at friends who were getting married younger than we and checking ourselves for problems, when, in reality, while we are *constantly* in a state of growing and maturity as we walk with Christ, marriage is not only for the perfect among us. If that were so, none of us would ever get married.

Here's another: "I can't understand why Mary is still single! She is such an amazing woman of God!"

Again, I'm reminded of someone I know. This young lady was twenty-nine when she met the young man that she would marry. She was amazing—a real Proverbs 31 woman in action. Her days were full of ministry to her family and her community, and she was a beautiful example of joyful contentment during singleness.

She was also a stay-at-home daughter who had endured many a snide remark from friends and family members who had assumed that the reason she was devoting herself to furthering her family's vision was so that she could rope a husband at the tender age of eighteen. As the years passed, they looked at her life and saw failure. My friend handled it well. She knew that the reason she was serving at home was to serve the Lord, and, as an extension of her service to him, to serve her family and to serve her community from home. And now, just a few short days from this writing, she will be marrying the man that the Lord was preparing for her all along (the man who the Lord was preparing in so many ways when she was my age). On those days when she felt lonely or discontent, God was moving in her life and in her future husband's life in ways she couldn't even fathom.

My friend was faithful, and she was content to serve where the Lord had placed her. Ever since I met her, I've been thinking in those "ten year" terms I talked about at the beginning of this section of the book: How can I serve the Lord for the next ten years? How can I serve without trying to "hold out" for marriage? How can I serve the Lord right now, keeping my eyes trained on him as he reveals his plan for my life?

If you are staying home as some sort of ticket to matrimony, I suggest you reevaluate your priorities. The goal for us unmarried daughters should be to bring glory to Christ in every season of our lives, not to strive to get married so that we can *start* giving him glory. This in no way undermines the beauty of marriage or the nobility of motherhood, but it does put the focus on the one who makes marriage beautiful, and who makes mothering worthwhile—he's the same King who makes our singleness worthwhile as we use it as a time to reflect on his goodness.

When Am I Ready for Marriage?

Part of what will help us view these years of singleness in proper perspective is not to see ourselves as packaged products on a shelf, ready to be snatched by the perfect man whenever he comes along. It can be so easy to throw up our hands and sigh about being "ready" for marriage without truly understanding that one is never really ready to be a bride until the Lord sends a bridegroom. Until then, we never run out of things that we can learn and do.

I know what it's like to want to mark off a checklist. I am definitely a checklist kind of girl. Not that I am a particularly organized person (painfully quite the opposite; in fact, that's one of the things I need to work on during these single years), but when I was in primary school, I always liked my mom to have a lesson plan, something I could look at infrequently, checking my progress. When I pack, I often make a list (toothbrush—check; soap—check; tee shirt—check; et cetera). I like being able to look back at my list and see a nice, neat row of black checkmarks marching across the page—it gives me a sense of satisfaction.

But one checklist I have trouble keeping track of is the checklist for marriage. You know, the mental checklist a lot of girls like me keep, girls who are striving to become capable wives of visionary husbands someday (especially when the "someday" often equals "as soon as possible"). It can get confusing, because "cooking skill" is easier to check off a list than "kindness." And does one have to be a gourmet, or is Hamburger Helper satisfactory? And, I mean, just how *kind* do I have to *be* anyway?

Does a girl ever reach a plan of "readiness?" Is she put on a shelf, if you will, after the age of eighteen or twenty-one, packaged, processed, and ripe for the taking? And if the gentleman shoppers neglect to procure her after ten years, is she taken off the shelf and given the gift of singleness? Do twenty-eight-year-old maidens have an expiration date after which they are put on the spinster aisle?

These questions may sound foolish to you, but think, for a moment, about how you view marriage. Are you so busy drowning your woes in bitter longing that you can't see your single years for the beautiful stage that they are to glorify the Lord in an exciting context? Why do we so often see our single years as "shelf years" anyway?

Enjoying Your Single Years

Here's another idea: Why don't we enjoy our single years?

Perhaps my outlook is a little sunny, not having been of "marriageable age" for very long, but bitterness hasn't quite struck me yet. At twenty, I am not quite considered a spinster by most peoples' terms—and even if you are reading this at age thirty and unmarried, you are on God's timetable. So let's stop looking at this time in our lives as The Longing Season and decide to look at it as The Growing Season.

Instead of wringing our hands in helpless, lonely melancholy, or conversely, allowing ourselves to become distracted and discouraged by the list of things we *must* achieve before we can get married, as if marital preparation were some sort of checklist that we could mark off with a gold sticker awaiting us at the end (enter: tall, dark, and handsome), let's understand that, while honest evaluation of our level of growth can sober and spur us onward as we mature in Christ, that maturity in Christ is the goal here—not matrimony.

You could be married nine months from now, or you could be married nine years from now. The Lord might purpose for you never to marry. There is no way that you can know exactly when or to whom you will wed. But here's what we do know: The Lord has given us life, perhaps an unmarried one at this point, and he has given us a mission to carry out, single or married (Matthew 28:18-20), and is constantly sanctifying us, single or married, and has called us to a purpose, single or married. . . .

And that's a wonderful thing!

I am not suggesting that we should not actively prepare to be capable wives and mothers... but daughterhood is the best training ground. Checklists aside, yes, we should have goals in mind, but not superficial goals that will crumble and waver with every unmarried year that passes. Our goals should be spiritual ones, ones that we can strive for whether we are getting married next year or getting married ten years from now, goals that can serve the Lord if he calls us to a life of singleness or whether we end up having eight children. Our goal should be to bless others in whatever sphere of influence the Lord has placed us—in whatever context he has called us to live out the biblical womanhood that he has called us to. For me, and for you, right now, perhaps that sphere is unmarried daughterhood.

Singleness. Which, for this "home girl" means a life being part of a covenant community of believers, fellowshipping with them, serving them, being discipled by them; living at home, serving my family, battling alongside them for God's glory, watching my adorable little brothers grow, and growing myself, under the patient eye of my parents. I'm really not so single, if you think about it. There's too much that can occupy my time, right where I am, for me to start pining over where I could be just yet.

Ever since I was a little girl, I have had a heroine that reminds me of just what a pivotal place I have in my home: Corrie Ten Boom. What I love about her life is that she was a true "1 Corinthians 7" woman (if there is such a thing!). She used her single years to bless her family, first in as small a way as helping around the house and helping her father run his business, and, later, by caring for her elderly relatives. She used her years of singleness to bless her community, first, by showing hospitality to strangers and blessing others through her various ministries, then, by harboring Jewish fugitives and protecting them from the Gestapo. Her single years went on and on... until death at a ripe, old age. But when I look at her life, I don't see a "waste". I see a fantastic woman who loved the Lord with a devotion that I want to possess. I see a woman I can't wait to spend a bit of eternity getting to know.

To spend my unmarried years discontentedly counting the moments until I'm married—if I marry—missing out on all of the blessings and opportunities the Lord has provided for me here and now, for his glory . . . *that* would truly be a waste.

What I want to do—and what I want to encourage you to do—is to trust in the Lord's sovereign timing as you look towards the future. That's something I want to talk about in a bit more detail in the next chapter.

CHAPTER ELEVEN

Overcoming a False View of God's Sovereignty & Embracing the Bigger Picture

Putting Desires in Proper Perspective

"I desire to get married, so I know that I will!"

"The Lord does not give us more than we can bear, and I am not wired for a life of singleness, so I will get married."

"I just feel that the Lord has called me to be married, so I will."

These sentiments (and variations of these sentiments) have all been uttered to me at one point or another by young women who desire to get married. They have been uttered by sixteen-year-olds who are convinced that the Lord will send them a husband by their eighteenth birthday. They have been uttered by twenty-eight-year-olds who just know that the Lord would not call them to be single in their thirties. They have been uttered by young women in their thirties who have become embittered towards the Lord because he has not kept his promise to give them the desires of their hearts.

In so many ways, this issue is the crux of discontentment. This is why I worry when I see a young woman at the tender age of eighteen becoming despondent because no one has asked for her hand in marriage yet. She is worried that something is wrong with her, and that this silence will set the pattern for years to come. I worry for the girl ten years her senior, who has had men come and go, but does not think any of them have been the right man for her. She is wondering if she should settle for the next guy that asks her, because, let's face it, she's not getting any younger. I worry for the girl who knows a young man that she would jump at the chance to marry, if only he would glance at her. She is turning down perfectly acceptable, godly young men because of the *one* guy whose attention she can't get, and she's perfectly convinced that God will send her the one she wants.

You know what? I worry for *myself* when I go through the very same emotions, and pray that those emotions always bring me to my knees and not to despondency.

Setting Ourselves Up for Disappointment

Why am I writing about contentment?

Is it because I've reached a plane of righteousness far beyond my unmarried sisters in Christ? Because I've understood timeless truths that they've never grasped before? Because I must impart the secret of my unwavering contentment? Because I'm a self-satisfied self-help guru who has all of the answers?

Nothing could be further from the truth. I am writing this because I'm a single girl like you. Just entering my twenties, I know what it's like to daydream about Prince Charming arriving atop his trusted steed (except in my case, it's average-Joe Johnny driving up in his Mustang). I haven't quite lost hope that Johnny's somewhere in the future. After all, I'm hardly decrepit. I am not arguing that godly young women will not have moments of battling with discontentment. But I *am* arguing that it should be a *battle!* So many of us have given up fighting. We have accepted discontentment as the status quo. And while I know that many of us receive encouragement from our mothers, fathers, and mentors, I want to offer a bit of encouragement as someone who doesn't "remember all to well" what it's like to be in that single season—she's still right there with you.

"It's natural for girls to feel this way," we have told ourselves. "My friends certainly do. If we could just get married, this feeling would go away!" And then we turn around and say, "I serve a sovereign King! If it's his will for me to be married, he'll send the right man along at the right time!"

I remember talking to a group of young ladies about marriage once, and stepping on top of my contentment soap box (which, I will admit, I keep quite handy). All of the people in the circle at the time were under twenty, and I asked, "How many of you would be completely crushed if you didn't end up getting married within the next five years?"

One young lady, instead of answering my question, tossed her head. "My mom was married at nineteen," she bragged.

"Mine was twenty-three," I shared.

"Mine was twenty-four," another young lady said.

The first young lady shrugged, a superior air hanging about her. "I've always thought I would get married young."

"A young marriage isn't promised to you just because your mom got married young," I pointed out. "Maybe the Lord's will for her is completely different for you."

"My mom says that I'm twice as ready as she was to get married when she was my age," the young lady maintained, ever smug.

"I get that," I replied. "But, really, aren't you *ready* to be married when the Lord says you're ready? I've known eighteen-year-olds who got married and could run the whole house, and twenty-four-year-olds who got married and couldn't boil water."

"Yes, but ..."

The conversation went around and around for a good five minutes. In the end, I was unable to convince this acquaintance that marriage any later than nineteen was a viable option for her. She never really spoke to me again after that, obviously put out with me for our conversation.

My friend, whose mother had been married a little later, looked at me when the dust cleared and smiled. "You're never too old to get married when you're waiting on God's timing," she said. I smiled. How true.

All I could think about whenever I thought about the conversation I had with the girl who had wanted to be married by the time she was nineteen—

and similar conversations I've had with other young ladies since then—was that, part of me hoped that she *did* get married at nineteen. Because if she didn't, she was going to be very angry with God; and part of me hoped that she didn't, so that she would learn that God has his own timetable. In pinning her hopes on a certain number, she was setting herself up for failure. She was setting herself up for pride and false theology ("I wanted this so much and in such the right way that God just gave it to me.") if she got married at a young age. And if the Lord called her to wait, she was setting herself up for bitterness.

How many of us are setting ourselves up for failure by setting superficial marriage goals and treating the Lord's sovereign will like a drive-through window?

Truly Trusting the Lord

In so many ways, understanding this point is solving the root of our discontentment problem: We don't truly trust in the Lord's sovereignty. While it's easy to say, "I trust the Lord to bring me a husband in his sovereign timing," it's harder to live those words out—to live, day by day, joyfully trusting in him. And while we might pretend to hold our dreams in open palms instead of clenched fists, and our lips may be saying, "I trust the Lord's sovereign will," our hearts scream out at the possibility that his sovereign will may not include a spouse in the near future—or at all. We "trust God's sovereign will" on our own terms: If he gives us what we want, he's a good and loving God; if what we want doesn't end up aligning with his will, we play the blame game.

And instead of turning to him for comfort, we turn to a daydream. Whether your dream proposal includes Dean Martin crooning *Volare* while you sail through Venice on a gondola or you're thinking you'd like to go the Hollywood route and get proposed to in the rain on your front porch (talk about cliche), our desire for marriage becomes the seat of our emotions. Our every waking thought is directed towards *someday*, and we lose sight of *today*. Worse, we lose sight of the Author of today. And yet we still expect him to satiate our longing for an idea that has become an idol.

Delighting Ourselves in the Lord

Delight yourself in the Lord, and he will give you the desires of your heart. —Psalm 37:4

So many of us disregard the first part of that passage and cling hungrily to the second. "He will give me the desires of my heart!" If I desire a husband, I'll get one, because husbands are good things, my God is a good God, my God is able, and he will not withhold my desires from me! We completely miss the command in that promise: *delight yourself in the Lord.* Which entails placing our desires at the foot of the cross. Which means placing our hope and trust solely in him—squarely in his hands. And when we trust the Lord will all of our hearts (Proverbs 3:5), when we entrust our desires to him, what we most wish for would be that *his will be done,* even if his will for us does not include marriage. It's a lesson we'll have to embrace throughout our lives, even if we get married tomorrow: Truly trusting God's sovereignty means letting go of our plans in light of his will.

This attitude of contentment is radically different from the attitude that walks around, despondent and forlorn, angry at God like a two-year-old gets angry at her parents because she isn't allowed to eat ice cream for breakfast. You see, the child's parents have insights that the child does not have. Eating ice cream for breakfast every morning is an unhealthy habit. Ice cream will not give her the nutrients she needs to grow healthy and strong. From the two-year-old's perspective, her parents are just being sadistic. From the parental perspective— the more knowledgeable perspective—they are actually being loving.

In the same way, we cannot see the panoramic view. All we can see is our myopic human perspective, when God sees so much more than we do. We stamp our foot and declare that we want to be married *right now* without stopping to consider that the Lord's plans are not our plans—that his ways are not our ways (Isaiah 55:6-11). We must do as we have been commanded to do, and we must trust the Lord to take care of the rest. He always does.

Choosing Contentment

One of my favorite books to read is *The Valley of Vision,* a collection of Puritan prayers. This particular prayer really blessed me this morning, and, in God's sovereign timing, I happened across it the very day I would be writing a chapter on contentment:

> *Heavenly Father, if I should suffer need, and go unclothed, and be in poverty, make my heart prize Thy love, know it, be constrained by it, though I be denied all blessings. It is Thy mercy to afflict and try me with wants, for by these trials I see my sins, and desire severance from them. Let me willingly accept misery, sorrows, temptations, if I can thereby feel sin as the greatest evil, and be delivered from it with gratitude to Thee, acknowledging this as the highest testimony of Thy love.*

> *When thy Son, Jesus, came into my soul instead of sin He*

became more dear to me than sin had formerly been; His kindly rule replaced sin's tyranny. Teach me to believe that if ever I would have any sin subdued I must not only labour to overcome it, but must invite Christ to abide in the place of it, and He must become to me more than vile lust had been; that His sweetness, power, life may be there. Thus I must seek a grace from Him contrary to sin, but must not claim it apart from Himself.

When I am afraid of evils to come, comfort me by showing me that in myself I am a dying, condemned wretch, but in Christ I am reconciled and live; that in myself I find insufficiency and no rest, but in Christ there is satisfaction and peace; that in myself I am feeble and unable to do good, but in Christ I have ability to do all things. Though now I have His graces in part, I shall shortly have them perfectly in that state where Thou wilt show Thyself fully reconciled, and alone sufficient, efficient, loving me completely, with sin abolished. O Lord, hasten that day.[12]

Talk about the opposite of entitlement! How we have lost our view of who we are in the grand scheme of things! Instead of sitting up and *demanding* things from the Lord, we should remember that we are but "dying, condemned [wretches]" who have already been given so very much from Christ, and who already have so much to be grateful for in him!

This doesn't mean that I don't pray for the desires of my heart. I do. But I pray that my heart would find solace in his plans, and not my own. May all of our desires stem from the love that should guide our every step (Matthew 22:37). May we fill our minds with things that turn our hearts towards Christ, and not the things that feed our flesh. This is not an all-out ban on Mr. Darcy, but if watching your most beloved chick flick makes you more anxious about your desires and less focused on the things you can do for Christ in the here and now, perhaps it's best to put it aside.

I trust in the Lord's sovereignty. More than that, I delight in the plan he's set forth for my life—I find my joy and fulfillment living in the very center of his will. Even when that means surrendering my will to his plans. Because the Lord knows what's best for me. He knows where I need to be to live out my life's purpose—to glorify him and enjoy him forever—to the very fullest. And wherever that is—married or single, single for a season or single for a lifetime—I trust him. And it's not by my own power that I do so. It's only by his grace that I'm able to trust him.

Do you?

Putting Dreams in Their Place

When I was a little girl, my brother and I used to sit around and talk about how many kids we wanted to have when we grew up. Trey had always settled on eight. I wanted nine. For most of my childhood, I was the oldest of two children, but Trey and I both wanted big families when we grew up. We were so close, we imagined that our kids would have even more fun together if there were more of them running around.

Little girl dreams of growing up to be a mommy were soon supplanted by more "mature" aspirations of the high calling of career. By the time I was fourteen, I was quipping that my spiritual gift was singleness, that I would never get married, and that, although I loved children, I would be okay not to have any of my own. Even after I decided to live at home after graduation, to serve my family and to reap the benefits of being part of a covenant community of believers at my church, I remember talking to one of my mom's closest friends (who, as I have gotten older, has become my friend as well) and telling her that I wondered if I had been given the gift of singleness.

The truth was, I had been around a lot of young women who had the same aspirations I was adopting. They were plugging into the family unit in order to reap the benefits of the protection, discipleship, and training that the home could afford a young lady. And they were also becoming so eager to snag a husband that they were not being faithful in ministering to the families that they had been given. I was actually worried that something was wrong with me—at seventeen, with three younger brothers ages 14, 3, and an infant, running my father's online business, working fulltime as his research assistant, keeping up research projects of my own, and, principally, helping my mom by serving in my home, it seemed to be that I had plenty of things to keep me busy without longing for a husband.

My friend gave me a knowing look. Because the concept of serving my family in this capacity was so new to me, she knew that I was still basking in the glow of my newfound contentment. "I can't imagine that you won't have some days ahead when you long just as much as the young women you're talking about. Bide your time."

She was right. Later on, she gave me this sage advice:

"Someday, you'll be married—and when you look back on those single years—even if they stretch longer than average—chances are, you'll spend more time married than you did as a single woman anyway. How did you use that *sliver* of time you had, the sliver you thought would stretch onto eternity some days, but ended up vanishing in the twinkling of an eye?"

Getting Exactly What You've Asked For

As the years have passed, I have reflected many times on that advice. It made me think of the worst punishment I ever received. I had been a complete brat after not getting my way (at an age where complete bratiness—better relegated to a tempestuous two-year-old—was "outdated," to say the least). My parents admonished me, and I was utterly humiliated by my immature behavior... and then my dad turned around and gave to me what I had been so anxious to receive.

As you can probably imagine, the gift wasn't as sweet.

That's how I view contentment. Marriage is a beautiful gift, and if it's what God has in store for us, it will come in his good timing. No amount of pouting and moping will make it get here faster. In fact, if we pout and mope, not only are we sinning in our lack of joy, but we're also losing precious years that could be used in full-hearted service to Christ.

This is something I'm passionate about because it's something I know. It hits me where I live the same way it might hit you. My friend was right—those longing days *did* come. But she was also correct in admonishing me to rise above them, to treat them like I would any other area of sin in my life, at times, to mortify the idol of marriage that I'd built as what it was: A flesh-centered desire that superseded my desire to serve God in the capacity that he had already blessed me with.

There are not ten easy steps to grounded contentment when all you can think about is a home and a hearth all your own. There is no magic pill you can take on those hard days when you gaze towards the horizon, straining your eyes to see the speck that may be Prince Charming finally looming there. There is nothing I can say that will forever eradicate the longing you have for wifehood.

Eradicating a Longing

And I don't think that longing necessarily needs to be eradicated.

You may be doing a double take right now. For six chapters, I've been extolling the virtues of remaining joyfully single, and now I'm backtracking and telling you to desire marriage? "Make up your mind, girl! You're giving me whiplash!"

We ought to be content in whatever state the Lord has placed us in, of course. But I do not believe that desiring marriage in its true context leads to discontentment. Desiring marriage so much that we lose sight of the blessing of singleness is a problem. Desiring marriage so much that we develop an unrealistic perception of it is a problem. Desiring marriage so much that we set it up as an idol to be worshiped instead of a state of service to the Lord is a problem. Desiring marriage so much that if we realize that it may not be what God has planned for us, we become embittered is a problem. Desiring the white dress, the pomp, the daydream and not truly understanding what marriage entails is a problem.

Desiring marriage as yet another means to glorify God? Desiring it in the sense that we are constantly pursuing God's will in that area, trusting him and not our own understanding as we wait for his plan to be revealed?

That, to me, is a beautiful thing.

And that's why, even at the closing of this section, I can still say, "I desire to be married." Not with a frown creasing my brow because my life is worthless without marriage or with a wistful sigh on my lips because life will be perfect once I'm married, but with my identity, my trust, and my hope firmly in Christ's hands. Praying fervently that his will be done in my life, single or married. Praying for joy in this journey, whether it includes marriage or not. Praying that, if it be his will, wifehood and motherhood would be around the corner eventually—that Johnny's on his way, whether his journey from Ireland (or, you know... wherever he is) is a lengthy one or a short one. That whether I'm married at twenty-two or thirty-two, I can embrace the life the Lord has given me day by day, not frittering away the years in wasted worry. That if I never get married, I can still encourage other young women to live their lives with contentment—with joy—with *gusto!*—as they delight in the plan of their Maker, which is perfect—whether it includes wedding bells or not.

Discontentment as a Sin

In his book, *Respectable Sins*, author Jerry Bridges speaks about a host of every day sins that we Christians tend to take lightly. In his chapter about discontentment, Dr. Bridges writes:

> *Whatever situation tempts us to be discontent, and however severe it may be, we need to recognize that discontentment is a sin. That statement may surprise many readers. We are so used to responding to difficult circumstances with anxiety, frustration, or discontentment that we consider them normal reactions to the varying vicissitudes of life. But if we tend to think this way, that just points out the subtleness and*

acceptability of these sins. When we fail to recognize these responses to our circumstances as sin, we are responding no differently from unbelievers who never factor God into their situations. We are back to our ungodliness as the root cause of our sins.[13]

He goes on to say:

Acceptance [the opposite of discontentment] means that you accept your circumstances from God, trusting that He unerringly knows what is beset for you and that in His love, He purposes only that which is best. Having then reached the state of acceptance, you can ask God to let you use your difficult circumstances to glory Him. In this way, you have moved from the attitude of a victim to an attitude of stewardship. You begin to ask, "God, how can I use my disability (or whatever the difficult circumstance may be) to glorify You?"

You may ask, "But shouldn't I pray for physical healing or for relief from any other painful circumstance?" Yes, we are invited to pray about these circumstances, but we should always pray in confidence that our infinitely wise and loving heavenly Father knows what is best for us, and we should be willing to accept his answer for us.[14]

Dr. Bridges writes these words as a man who has experienced the crushing blow of losing his first wife. He writes in the face of devastation that many of us can never imagine. Yet, even in the midst of great sorrow in his past, he is able to encourage us to see discontentment for what it is: a distraction from trusting in the glorious provision of our King.

He does offer this disclaimer:

. . . I want to acknowledge that there is a place for legitimate discontentment. All of us should, to some degree, be discontent with our spiritual growth. If we are not, we will stop growing. There is also what we might call a prophetic discontentment with the injustice and other evils in society that is coupled with the desire to see positive change. The subject of his chapter is a sinful discontentment that negatively affects our relationship with God.[15]

As we grow in grace, as we pinpoint the sin of discontentment in our lives, including the sin of discontentment, we are able to put our longings in proper perspective, and to lean on the Lord as he causes spiritual growth to spring in our lives.

There is a difference between praying to God for the desires of our hearts—and setting those desires up as an idol in our lives. One of them keeps the focus on the all-wise provision of the King of Kings, the other puts the focus on the desires themselves.

How Do I Tell the Difference Between Acceptance and Discontentment?

If I desire marriage for marriage's sake, then I wring my hands in melancholy every day that goes by without producing a husband; I question God's love for me when he does not send me one as soon as I'd like to have him, and I cannot see a purpose outside of becoming a wife and mother.

If I truly desire marriage because I want to bring glory to the Lord in that way . . . then I realize that if the Lord's plan for me doesn't include marriage, there is another way that I can better bring him glory. He created me with that purpose in mind.

I am not always as grounded or focused a single person as I would like to be. Who knows? I may have years of practice ahead of me to refine the skill. But as I travel on this journey, I'm reminded that contentment is a daily battle and a daily choice. Seeking out the blessings in the here and now is difficult when we're bogged down with a fanciful perception of what the future will hold. It's easier to do when we have a firmer grasp on the bigger picture: God's glory. Married or single, we're always after the same thing.

Part Three

CHAPTER TWELVE

Why Do You Live at Home?

When I first wrestled with the decision to stay at home after high school, I thought the hardest part of coming home would be reevaluating the dreams and hopes and plans I had pinned on my college education. I thought that once I came to terms with the new set of goals that I had set for myself, and found my niche in serving my family, the battle would be over.

Little did I know that my immediate family and I were not the only ones who had to come to terms with my decision. Extended family members, friends, and even strangers felt that they had the right to comment one way or another on the choice I made, and to offer (often unsolicited) commentary on my lifestyle.

When I started blogging, things got worse. On the one hand, a blog is a public forum—those who write do so at their own risk. However, it never ceases to amaze me how people who are diametrically opposed to my lifestyle curiously peruse what I write. I always liken it to a young conservative evangelical like myself religiously reading the blog of a left-wing homosexual college student. Frankly, that's just not something I would do. My curiosity has its limits.

What I soon learned, however, was that the curiosity of others often doesn't seem to have those limits. We who have chosen to forgo the typical post-high school experience are leading a countercultural existence. Our choice to remain under our father's protection, in submission to our parents, and to constantly benefit from their discipling after high school instead of heading cross-country to attend a university with career plans in mind and independence at heart is counter-intuitive to most American families, more so, even, than Christian education and discipleship during primary schooling, choosing to attend a family integrated church, or choosing to abandon the modern dating scene. It's understandable that onlookers—believers and non-believers alike—should be curious.

Questions range from the guileless ("So, what does your average day look like—what are your long-term goals?") to the loaded ("So, when your dad unlocks the chain on your cage in the basement, how much give do the shackles on your ankles have?"). Seriously. That second one isn't much of a stretch. For some critics, "I chose not to take the traditional route to post-high school education" becomes "I don't believe women should be well-educated." "I value emotional purity" becomes "I'm not allowed to talk to boys, and have to avert my eyes in their presence." "I trust my parents' oversight and guidance as we partner in the courtship process" becomes "My marriage has been arranged since I was two, and my only part in the courtship process is to say 'I do' at the altar."

Think I'm exaggerating?

Several months ago, I wrote an article called *A People Pleaser* in response to quite a few anonymous comments I'd been receiving on my blog. Here's one of them:

> *I'm sad for you. You have been entirely brainwashed. Hopefully, you'll grow up and leave your abusive church.*
>
> *When you do, you will see how horrific your father's ideas are. You seem like a bright young woman. Sigh.*[16]

In *People Pleaser*, I talked about the importance of answering questions from outsiders with grace and dignity, even when we are not afforded the same courtesy. Little did I know, the comment section would offer me an opportunity to practice what I preach:

> *Dear Jasmine,*
>
> *"Brainwashed," is an archaic term. A more accurate description for someone in your position is a phenomenon known as*

Stockholm Syndrome. It was originally observed in kidnap victims who, over time, became sympathetic to their captors, and a similar phenomenon has been observed in many women and children living in religiously fundamentalist patriarchal households and societies (Islamic and Christian sects alike). It's a survival mechanism, not a personality or intellectual deficit.

Please know, no matter what, YOU ARE a survivor. Remain steadfast and strong knowing God—the true God—is working through people in this country and throughout the world to prevent women and children from being subjected to the religious perversions imposed upon you.

God Bless,
Julie

I couldn't make this stuff up. Every question I will mention in this section is one that I have been asked, sometimes kindly and patiently by well-meaning Christians, and sometimes rudely by lesser well-meaning folk.

Just last night, we had dinner guests, and a thirteen-year-old who I had seen briefly on a number of occasions walked up to me and asked how old I was.

"Twenty," I replied.

She looked flabbergasted. "Yeah, right. You're twenty?"

I laughed, thinking she had made the mistake that so many others make about me. I'm often mistaken for a fifteen-year-old, which I'm told will come in handy the older I get. Being a very indignant twenty, I'm not so sure yet! So I reassured her of my age.

"Wow. I didn't know some twenty-year-olds weren't out on their own making something of themselves and going to college—you're just living at home!"

I didn't flinch, although I might have three years ago. I'm used to that reaction.

Because we are in the minority, we are going to need to learn to anticipate the wide variety of questions that are going to come our way. The simplest question that anyone can ask us is *why.*

Why did you choose to stay at home? Why aren't you off at college? Why aren't you pursuing a college education?

Isn't that what everyone else is doing?

We live in a culture that claims to be strongly individualistic and unfailingly tolerant. However, in truth, for a young woman to wander off the path so carefully beaten for her by generations of young women who have forsaken the ministry of the home is taboo. Even in our extremely "tolerant" culture, some decisions—usually those that flow from biblical conviction—are considered off-limits.

So how do we explain ourselves when inquiring minds what to know? How do we answer the question that is sure to come: *Why*?

Perhaps you are reading this book, and you know *of* stay at home daughterhood, but aside from what you've read on the Internet or heard via secondhand information, you have never actually seen one in action. Maybe you know a stay-at-home daughter, and you are considering coming home yourself. Maybe you're a stay-at-home daughter who has been asked this question a thousand times, and you can't think of a succinct answer.

First, you have to understand for yourself why it is you live at home before you can articulate it to other people. Is it because staying home until you get married was something you were always taught, and something that you learned to take for granted? Is it because you never really had any ambition outside of living at home, and so it seemed natural to stay there when you were done with high school? Maybe you have a friend who decided to do it, so you decided to give it a try yourself.

The fact is, none of these reasons are quite good enough. The guiding reason for whatever we do should be to bring glory to Christ—this goes from our day to day conduct to as big a decision as how we will spend our time once we have graduated high school. In this spirit, living at home after graduation should be a decision that we can trace back to guiding principles in God's Word.

The *why* question comes in many forms, and I will try to tackle many of them in this chapter. When I am done, however, I'm sure there will be some variations I have missed. What I hope to portray here is not that you should run and pick up this book whenever you receive a hard question and thumb its pages for a viable answer. My aim is to arm you with some confidence as you come up with answers for yourself.

As another note, I have received each one of these questions and accusations either in person or via my blog, sometimes in ruder forms than they appear here. If nothing else, staying at home will definitely teach you the importance of having a thick skin about criticism. I know it's definitely helped me!

Question # 1: So what college are you going to?

A: I'm actually not going off to school.

Be prepared for an awkward silence as your listener tries to come up with a polite way to say, "What do you *mean* you're not going to college? Are you a part of some cult?"

Be patient with your questioner. What you have just said flies in the face of the American dream. A little girl growing up in the West is presented with the all-American ideal as being sent to the high-profile college of her dreams, where all of her desires will be easily within her grasp as long as she can present the golden ticket: her diploma. A college diploma is insurance against poverty. A young woman is told that if she is educated enough, she can get a good enough job to ensure that she will never be financially insecure again. A college diploma is an insurance against dependency. A young woman is told that she will be fully self-sufficient with the right amount of education and work experience. A college diploma is insurance against bigotry: Little girls can fight the tide of sexism by proving that they are just as well-educated as the men in their lives.

A college diploma is what sets the women of today apart from the Suzie Homemakers of the Stone Age. It has gone beyond being a cosmopolitan status symbol: It's required.

Now, I didn't know the depths of this requirement until I started blogging. In the anonymous world of the Internet, people started to drop the sugar coating when they talked about my blog, and I have gotten my fair share of hurtful e-mails, comments, and incoming links that betray that, in some people's minds, "I'm actually not going off to school," is translated like this: "I have chosen to give up my American birthright. I desire to revert back to a time when women were treated like property because it is a safe little bubble wherein I will be a cosseted ornament to society who never uses her God-given gifts and talents outside of the paradigm of housework."

In others' minds, it may just register as confusion: "There's another way to do things?"

You didn't know one sentence could communicate so much, did you?

If you are going to give up the American dream, be prepared to answer *why* it is you have decided to do so. Here's the *why* for me:

The American dream failed to line up with my biblical calling as a woman, as a daughter, and as someone who may—and probably will—become a wife someday. Glean God's Word as I might, I can see no pattern in Scripture for a young woman to pack up and head cross-country to be discipled outside of the framework of the church and home.

Question #2: So do you want to go back to the days where women were treated like property to be passed from father to husband?

A: I want to go "back" to Scripture and Scripture alone.

When I read God's Word, in passages like Numbers 30, and when I read Jeremiah 29 and other passages that speak about the giving of a daughter in marriage, I do not see women being treated like property. What I see is the beautiful provision and protection that they have been afforded in the Scriptures. Allowing your dad to carry out his God-given duty to provide for you is not a sign of weakness or intellectual flabbiness anymore than following any other imperative in the Bible is.

I do not deny that there were instances in times gone by when women were treated like property. Where I disagree is that God's Word is the culprit for this mistreatment. Nothing could provide a woman with a higher status than to understand the security the Lord has given her in the family unit, as a daughter in her father's home first, and then as a wife. Genesis 2 shows us that woman was created with her highest calling in mind: Mankind was incomplete without her.

I believe that egalitarianism mars the beautiful symmetry between mankind and womankind by eradicating the difference between them. In her book, *Girls Gone Wise in a World Gone Wild*, which I mentioned in a previous chapter, Marry Kassian describes the difference this way:

> *The Lord created woman with a bent to be amenable,*
> *relational, and receptive. He created man with a bent to*
> *initiate, provide, and protect. As we talked about in an earlier*
> *chapter, Genesis 3:16 indicates that sin severely damaged the*
> *God-given inclination of both. Sin twisted the positive desire of*
> *women to respond amenably to man into a negative desire to*
> *resist and rebel against him. It twisted the positive drive of man*
> *to use his strength to lead, protect, and provide for woman into*
> *a negative tendency to abuse or refuse that responsibility.*[17]

We need to let go of this desire to prove ourselves to the men in our lives and realize that our true, guiding focus should be to prove ourselves true followers of Christ by obeying his Word. When we do so, it becomes much simpler for us to understand how beautiful the difference between men and women is, and how freeing it is to embrace our femininity.

Embracing biblical womanhood does not mean embracing the Susie Homemaker caricature in the back of your mind. When people think of "biblical femininity," I think that, in general, the image that pops into their minds is a flowery representation from yesteryear, resplendent with yards of lace and satin, ankle-length hair piled up to the heavens, china-doll faces, soft hands not used to labor. When they think of stay-at-home moms, the perfect Susie-homemaker pops into their head, complete with 1940s swing dress paired with peep-toe heels and flowery aprons.

Now, don't get me wrong; lace is all fine and good, and I like peep-toe heels as much as the next girl! But if we are going to be young women serious about biblical femininity, we need to have a clear perception of what biblical femininity actually *is*, not what our culture perceives it to be.

One thing I can tell you right off the bat is that it has very little to do with being a mere *ornament* to society, a porcelain doll or a caricature. How do I know this?

Looking at the woman of Proverbs 31:10-31, I see that biblical femininity is characterized by industry, by good stewardship, by competence, by prudence and hard work! I see a living picture of the command in Titus 2:3-5, a keeper at home in action who has little use for stilettos while she's doing housework.

This is not to say that biblical femininity isn't also characterized by beauty and grace. Also in Proverbs, we see again and again that husbands are commanded to *delight* in the wives of their youth; in Song of Songs, we see a beautiful picture of a woman who is attractive to her husband, whose beauty is something he is able to take pleasure in. Yet, by the same token, I'm reminded of a verse in Proverbs that says:

Like a gold ring in a pig's snout is a beautiful woman without discretion (Proverbs 11:22)

We see that biblical femininity is also characterized by a gentle and quiet spirit in 1 Peter 3:1-6, and by a submissive heart in Ephesians 5. Biblical femininity is not characterized by a quarrelsome spirit (Proverbs 21:9, 19; 25: 34; 19:13; 17:15), but by graciousness (Proverbs 11:16), and by a fear of the Lord (Proverbs 31:30).

While women were created differently from men, there are a host of biblical commands that apply to both women and men. The first one that always comes to is the command in Galatians 5 to walk by the spirit; a woman who is truly seeking "biblical womanhood" will be a woman who delights herself wholly in the Lord and in living out His commandments, in walking in His precepts.

I believe that men and women have complementary roles in creation, that God created Eve, not as an androgynous double of Adam, but as a helper suitable, and both women and men can delight in that difference. With that in mind, I think it behooves young women to sort through the generalizations and expectations of the culture around us and seek the heart of biblical womanhood, learning what it truly means to be a woman of God from His Word. It's not that easy. Embracing your femininity is more than wearing a pretty dress or putting on makeup. It starts with a heart that is submitted to the Lord's will, and a will that is bent towards his plan for your life. Until you truly understand that concept, this question is going to throw you for a loop.

Question #3: So you don't think that a woman should be self-sufficient?

A: I think that a woman should be incredibly competent, resilient, and reliable.

Independence seems to be looked upon as one of the best virtues a modern woman can possess. Gone are the days of being locked in that ivory tower, waiting for prince charming to arrive on his faithful steed; we'll climb down ourselves, thank you very much. Me, wait for a *man* to solve all of my problems? I've got this, sir; step aside. Biblical submission has been redefined as servitude, headship as chauvinism, and we women couldn't be happier for it, right?

I don't think we can lay all of the blame for this glorification of an independent spirit and staunch individualism at the feet of the feminism that has warped our understanding when it comes to male and female roles; I think equal, if not more blame, can be laid at the feet of the American way. We are a people known for our independence, lauded for our individualism, who balk at the idea of depending on someone else for anything, being beholden to anyone for anything (*unless that someone is the government, it seems, but I digress*).

Noah Webster's 1828 Dictionary defines independence as:

> *Not dependent; not subject to the control of others; not subordinate. God is the only being who is perfectly independent.*[18]

It defines dependence as:

Subject to the power of; at the disposal of; not able to exist or sustain itself without the will or power of. Thus, we are dependent on God and his providence; and effect may be dependent on some unknown cause.[19]

In this sense, none of us is truly independent; we are all dependent on the Lord. While we may like the idea that we are sovereign over our own actions, the fulfilling of our own desires, even the meeting of our most basic needs, when circumstances happen that are "outside of our control," we are reminded of the sovereignty of God, the Providence that touches all of our lives.

Being willing to give up that "independence" mindset does not mean that we give way to the ridiculous caricature of the soft-handed damsel in distress. Going back to the example of the woman in Proverbs 31:10-31, we do not see a woman who is incompetent and inept for the noble task of wifehood; however, we know that if she is said to do her husband "good and not evil all the days of his life" (Proverbs 31:11-12), then she is being submissive wife (Ephesians 5:22). To my modern sensibilities, when I first began to study them, these two pictures don't seem to mesh. On the one hand, you have a wife that is obviously industrious, strong, and competent, and on the other hand, you have a command that many assume means that women are expected to be the exact opposite!

But I was confusing competency with independence.

The wife is not independent of her husband; she is to submit to him, not because he is necessarily smarter or even more spiritual than she is (1 Peter 3:1-6); she is to submit to him as unto the Lord. This submission does mean letting go of her feigned independence (the independence that none of us can truly boast, since God is Lord over all things), but it does not mean that she is not *competent*.

Being competent is described in Webster's 1828 dictionary as:

Suitable; fit; convenient; hence, sufficient, that is, fit for the purpose; adequate; followed by to; as, competent supplies of food and clothing; a competent force; an army competent to the preservation of the kingdom or state; a competent knowledge of the world. This word usually implies a moderate supply, a sufficiency without superfluity.[20]

Suitable. Fit for the purpose. Adequate.

These are all words that remind me of the term: "helpmeet." A helper suitable.

JOYFULLY AT HOME: CHAPTER TWELVE

A suitable helper should be one of the most competent, intelligent, and driven women around. She should not be sitting around waiting for her every romantic whim to be filled, wringing her hands when asked to do something that she might not know how to do, set upon a shelf as something that is merely ornamental, but not useful. The home is her domain (Titus 2:3-5), and she should be able to run it smoothly and efficiently.

Question #4: But isn't being a helpmeet a job that only a wife and mother can do? What about 1 Corinthians 7:34?

A: Yes, being a helpmeet is something that only a wife can do.

But being a *helper* is something that is innate in womankind—it was what we were created for. While the nature of a young man is often seen as something fixed and transcendent—men are to be leaders, providers, protectors—the nature of womankind has been given a flimsier definition. If a woman is a wife, she is to be provided for, protected, and led—she is to be bent towards her home. If a woman is single, however, she is to be... a man with the potential to become a woman if ever she should marry.

This never bothered me until I sat down to think about it. Why is it that we accept biblical manhood in every context—single or married—and encourage men to strive towards the unchanging concept, while biblical womanhood is seen as something that can only truly be realized if we are married? That, if we are single women, our nature is completely different from that of a married woman?

> *And the unmarried or betrothed woman is anxious about the things of the Lord, how to be holy in body and spirit. But the married woman is anxious about worldly things, how to please her husband. —I Corinthians 7:34*

In the larger context, Paul is speaking to the Christians in the early church about the advantages of the gift of singleness (1 Corinthians 7:6-7) in the difficult days in which they lived. Imagine an era where Christians are being systematically rounded up and thrown to the lions, where children are being orphaned at such a rate that the early church's adoption ministry was bigger back then than anything we could imagine today, where taking up your cross to follow Christ *literally* meant giving your life if you were discovered.

I would that I remained as I was, a single woman who would not leave behind a family and children in such perilous times. But even in this chapter, the Apostle Paul acknowledges that singleness is a supernatural spiritual gift, not something that we can opt for at will.

We unmarried women are to be anxious about the things of the Lord. As we do not have husbands to care for, our hands are free to serve within the context of our homes and churches. Single women have been called "the secret weapon of the church," ready and willing to sacrifice their time and energy to aid those in need.

What woman has more time on her hands to minister to the church? The one with a full college course-load, who has devoted her time and energy into becoming an independent, autonomous agent? Or the one who has made it her life's ambition to cultivate the gifts and talents that will aid the brethren, should she remain single, and bless her home should she become a wife and mother?

My innocent conjecture would be that the latter would be more of an aid than the former.

There is a fifth question that might catch you offguard: "Are your parents making you do this?"

The short answer should be no. The Fifth Commandment is important to a daughter who has chosen to live at home, for she has chosen to submit herself to the rule and authority of her parents in a unique way that a daughter who has opted to move out on her eighteenth birthday has not. Because of the unique nature of this relationship, you will soon learn that it is constantly under fire. Your parents—your father in particular—will be painted as stifling villains, and you will have to endeavor to protect their reputation among those who disagree with your lifestyle.

Answer this particular question emphatically, because the honor of your parents is at stake. "I'm at home because I want to be. Because I realize the advantages of living under my father's protection and my mother's discipleship, and because I am so grateful that God's Word makes provision for the home to be such a thorough training ground for my future."

I am so grateful for the Lord's hand on my life for turning my heart towards home when I was inclined on a different path. If you find yourself struggling, as I did, with what may be a new emphasis by your parents on a daughter's place in the home, I would encourage you to go to the Scriptures for answers and show grace to your parents, even when they don't have all the details sorted out yet. When it all comes down to it, though we may be accused of being coddled and cosseted, our consciences need to be right before God. If that is the case, we have nothing to fear or to apologize for.

Of course, some questioners *are* going to try to instill fear in us with the constant barrage of *What if* questions, which I hope to cover in the next chapter.

CHAPTER THIRTEEN

But What If...?

I have to say, I'm not very fond of "what if" scenarios. And this is coming from a girl who is always pondering them. I am, after all, a fiction-writer and a film-lover—I get my kicks from "what if" scenarios. However, whenever they come in rapid-fire in real life situations, I'm always tempted to answer such inquiries a little sarcastically: "What if we all die tomorrow? What if a meteor hits the earth? What if Martians come and suck out our brains with straws? What if the well dries up?"

Philippians 4:5-6 says:

Let your reasonableness be known to everyone. The Lord is at hand; do not be anxious about anything, but in everything by prayer and supplication with thanksgiving let your requests be known to God.

Matthew 6:35 also reminds us not to "borrow trouble":

Therefore do not be anxious about tomorrow, for tomorrow will be anxious for itself. Sufficient for the day is its own trouble.

Luke 12:22-31 goes on to say:

And he said to his disciples, "Therefore I tell you, do not be anxious about your life, what you will eat, nor about your body, what you will put on. For life is more than food, and the body more than clothing. Consider the ravens: they neither sow nor reap, they have neither storehouse nor barn, and yet God feeds them. Of how much more value are you than the birds! And which of you by being anxious can add a single hour to his span of life? If then you are not able to do as small a thing as that, why are you anxious about the rest? Consider the lilies, how they grow: they neither toil nor spin, yet I tell you, even Solomon in all his glory was not arrayed like one of these. But if God so clothes the grass, which is alive in the field today, and tomorrow is thrown into the oven, how much more will he clothe you, O you of little faith! And do not seek what you are to eat and what you are to drink, nor be worried. For all the nations of the world seek after these things, and your Father knows that you need them. Instead, seek his kingdom, and these things will be added to you.

We are not to be given to a spirit of fear (1 Timothy 1:7), but of boldness in the certainty of our all-wise King's provision. Our anxiety is a sinful effort on our part to seek to control that which God has already established. Our fiercely independent society has trained us to think that we can somehow make provision against what God has already willed, and so, in an effort to micromanage the future, we young ladies are expected to have backup plan after backup plan after backup plan.

There is, however, a place for wise provision in light of God's sovereignty. James 4:13-24 says:

Come now, you who say, "Today or tomorrow we will go into such and such a town and spend a year there and trade and make profit"—yet you do not know what tomorrow will bring. What is your life? For you are a mist that appears for a little time and then vanishes. Instead, you ought to say, "If the Lord wills, we will live and do this or that."

James has just modeled for us the appropriate attitude in making plans for the future. In reliance to God, we carry out his commands. In confidence, we submit to the Lord's will even while we make provision for the future.

We Houstonians have the perfect example of the dichotomy between power of God and the plans of man: It's called hurricane season. Every year in the fall, we have at least one threat of a hurricane. If the hurricane blows through, no matter what plans we've made are put aside. Businesses close. Highways are congested. Property is destroyed. We are forced to seek shelter or sanctuary, depending on the power of the hurricane and the resources we have at hand.

We don't live in constant fear of hurricanes from June to October. We don't save wedding plans or business meetings or coastal vacations for November to May. We don't mourn a pregnant mother who's due date falls in August. We live our lives as we normally would, in spite of the threat of a storm.

In much the same way, we should approach *What if?* questions, not with fear and frustration, but constantly leaning in God's sovereignty, even as we make plans for the future.

Question #1: What if you never get married?

A: My usefulness at home is not contingent upon how old I am.

This question came to me from a reader of my blog several months ago. She wanted to know "whether if you don't get married by the time you're 30, will you stay at home when your brothers are grown up or will you take up some missionary work?"

Well, first off, my analytical eye caught several flaws in the question (perhaps *misconceptions* is a better word). I am not usually offended by these kinds of questions, as I realize my lifestyle seems wholly countercultural to most; therefore, I feel that it's necessary to correct misconceptions when I see them, in hopes of giving a better understanding.

The first assumption? That I won't be married by thirty. If I'm not married by twenty-six, I'll take arsenic and end my spinsterish misery. In fact, make that twenty-one. The countdown has begun. Because life is meaningless if Johnny isn't by my side.

Just kidding.

My first observation was the assumption that if I am not married at thirty, I shan't be married at all. Nothing could be further from the truth. This year has brought me so much news of courtships, engagements, and marriages of dear friends and acquaintances, ranging from age eighteen to age forty. It is amazing the things the Lord will do when we least expect them, and when we are willing to wait on his timing. Remember what we talked about in the last section? His timing is perfect.

Further, though, Lord willing, I would be very pleased to be married within the next few years to the visionary of my dreams, I realize that my life has a goal that is bigger than marriage. If I'm living my life in such a way now that I can't foresee being useful and content in the Lord's service single ten years down the line, then I'm wasting my time. Even if I get married a year from now, if this time at home is a time where I'm spinning my wheels and waiting for prince charming to come along, this time is neither productive nor profitable to my spiritual development. 1 Corinthians 7 gives these single year abundant meaning: I'm to be about the Lord's business.

Which brings me to my third observation: While the bulk of my time at home is, indeed, being employed helping and serving my family by wrangling my brothers (and I'm using "wrangling" as an affectionate term—you haven't lived until you've heard a houseful of boys squealing with laughter, the tramp of their feet barreling downstairs, the sounds of their many make-believe games, or the smiles that their simplest precious moments will bring to your face), that's not all I'm doing. When these boys of mine are gone, I'll still have plenty to occupy my time with my work for my dad's ministry, our family's ministry, and personal projects, as well as more spaces of time to be filled with ministry in our church and in the larger context of the body of believers. I'm so much more than a live-in nanny.

Aside from that, though, when I'm thirty (in 10 years), my brothers will be twenty-seven, fifteen, thirteen, eleven, and ten. There are six of us now; Lord willing, my father would like to have ten children before our adoption journey is over with. Mama and I got together and estimated that, if we keep going at our current rate, in ten years, I could have a sibling as young as five. At thirty, my big-sistering days will hardly be over; and, Lord willing, my oldest brother will supply me with aunty-ing days ahead. And, Lord willing, should marriage be in my future (and when I'm not in an overly cynical mood, I do believe it could be), I'm the girl who looks forward not so much to her wedding day as to being able to see my grandchildren and perhaps my great grandchildren walking with the Lord.

But, back to the original question:

I enjoy reading your work and was wondering whether if you don't get married by the time you're 30, will you stay at home when your brothers are grown up or will you take up some missionary work?

The answer is: I'm doing missionary work now. I'm an ambassador for Christ right here, in my home, among the brethren, among the culture that we live in. Living at home until I'm married is a choice that I've made because I want to be here... for as long as the Lord wills, doing whatever he calls me to do in this sphere, delighting in being wherever he calls my family, diligently serving in and through my home. It's a choice I've made based on the firm belief that it is the best and safest place for me to be until my father gives me in marriage to a provider, protector, prophet, and priest. Hardships included, I love it; at nineteen, there's nowhere else I'd rather be. At thirty, we'll see what the Lord has in store. I could be raising little boys who really are my very own (a girl, even), married to Johnny and ministering day-to-day at home, in the trenches—or I could be living at home, ministering in a different way, a published author perhaps, a piano teacher, an English tutor, the *best* big sister . . . or I could be doing something that I can't even fathom right now.

But I hope to be doing it in a family unit, whatever the case may be.

Question #2: What if your father or husband dies, or they are unable to provide for you because of an injury or illness?

A: What if the local church took its duty towards widows and orphans seriously?

What I once thought was a private question that I would only be asked by a few turned out to be an inquiry I receive quite often.

I know it's not polite to answer a question with a question, but think about it: While wills, life insurance policies, and detailed plans are all important measures that a father can use to ensure that their families are well provided for (and I have nothing against these methods, and know personally the security that they provide) (1 Timothy 5:8), so many of us miss out on the security that the Body of Christ should afford us.

> *If anyone thinks he is religious and does not bridle his tongue but deceives his heart, this person's religion is worthless. Religion that is pure and undefiled before God, the Father, is this: to visit orphans and widows in their affliction, and to keep oneself unstained from the world.—James 1:26-27*

The Church has a real responsibility towards widows and orphans, so much so that this responsibility is outlined in by the Apostle Paul in 1 Timothy 5. Have you ever taken a good, long look at that passage? Have you ever been in a church that has encouraged you to do so?

One of the biggest provisions that a father can make for his family is to get them to a doctrinally sound, biblically functioning church with a strong sense of community. If you live anywhere near Houston, Texas, I know one you can visit. But even if you don't happen to live in Texas, talk to your parents about making a solid church home a priority. They do exist.

Question #3: What if you don't attend a church that takes James 1:26-27 seriously? What if you need to work, and you don't have a job or a college degree? What if your husband gets laid off or injured and needs you to help pick up the slack?

A: A college degree is no substitute for the assurance we have in Christ.

Again, the degree is a piece of paper that provides us with a false sense of security. You would be surprised at how many times I have heard someone say, "You know, in this economy, it's really foolish not to get a college degree that will promote job security—I have three degrees, and I just got laid-off! What makes you think you'll be able to find a job when you need one?"

I have three degrees. . . . and I just got laid off.

They don't even realize that their sentence has revealed the faulty assurance they are offering you. If college degrees were a buffer against job-loss, then our three-degreed friend would not have gotten laid off.

This is not to say that getting a college degree is a sign of faithlessness; rather, that getting it out of a sense of fear is responding, not to the Lord's leading in that area, but to a cheap scare-tactic.

Question #4: What if you need a college degree to homeschool your children?

A: Define the word *need.*

Many stay-at-home daughters that I know are also young women who want to homeschool their children. Because they understand the importance of purity and protection in their own lives, they desire to provide their children with the same protection, not just after high-school, but throughout their entire educational experience. If you are not familiar with the benefits of homeschooling or the dangers of the public school system, I recommend *The Harsh Truth About Public Schools.* A debate about our mode of education is outside of the scope of this particular book, but this question bears mentioning.

In answer to the question: *Does a homeschool mom need a degree to teach her own children?* I have to utter a resounding *no!* And this comes from the daughter of a woman who graduated *magna cum laude* from one of the biggest historically black colleges in America with a teaching degree, and a father who likes to joke that he has "more degrees than a thermometer," and has experienced the rigorous academic environments of schools like Rice University here in the States and Oxford in England.

I firmly believe that the God who commanded parents to raise their children up in the nurture and admonition of the Lord (Ephesians 6:4, Deuteronomy 6) will fully equip them to do so, with or without an education in the indoctrination centers that many colleges have become (I say "many," because I still believe there are examples of biblically-operated colleges, and am ever refreshed by them). My mother has told me time and again that her education degree was not only unhelpful in her quest to homeschool my brothers and I, but detrimental—she wanted to teach her children to think outside the box—her education degree had given her the tools she needed to manage a classroom of thirty children while teaching them to walk in lockstep.

However, when the word *need* means that State law could begin to mandate certain certification for teaching, we are talking about a real threat to the homeschooling movement. While I live in a state that is very generous towards homeschoolers, I have watched over the years as other states have buckled down when it comes to regulations.

I believe that Christians should be very active in the political arena, protesting and voting against legislation like this, and aiding families who will be affected by it if it *does* pass; however, the fact still stands that, if the Lord should call me to a state like, say, New York, definite changes would have to take place in order for me to continue to homeschool prospective children the same way I would here in Texas.

Because these laws are a very real threat, the decision to get a college degree to promote homeschooling security should be one that you and your parents should make together. This decision does not negate the experience of living at home between high school graduation and marriage; on the contrary, I myself am in the process of working towards a fully accredited degree in English from the comfort of my home.

I decided to get the English degree for a number of reasons, homeschooling laws being an extremely peripheral one. For the most part, I was very interested in the online program being offered, and wanted to challenge myself in new ways. If homeschooling laws are your reason for getting a college education, though, I would strongly caution you; a nation that tries, constantly, to make it more and more difficult for homeschoolers, will not stop at legislation that would make it illegal for mothers to homeschool without a college degree; it's a slippery slope. I don't think any type of degree—even a doctorate in education—is a safety net against homeschool laws.

Question #5: What if something happens and I have to work. Is that a sin?

A: Again, this question can be answered with another question: how do you define "have" to work?

Are you defining the need in terms of the number of cars you want sitting in your garage, or in terms of putting food in your family's mouths?

Daddy has an excellent answer to this question in his book, *Family Driven Faith*:

> "... I am not saying that any mother who works outside the home is sinning. That is for each family to decide as they wrestle with the Scriptures and their circumstances. I know there are many mothers who have to work. My mother, like far too many women, was left to raise a child alone. She did not have the luxury of being a stay-at-home mom. My mother had to put food on the table.
>
> "Other women's husbands have died or are disabled. Some women have chosen career paths that allow them to work when their children are at school, and others work part-time as volunteers. All of this is in keeping with the Proverbs 31 woman...
>
> "The ultimate question, however, is, "Are we working because we have to or because we don't think our house is big enough or our car new enough or our bank accounts fat enough?" If it is the latter, we have crossed the line. That is when our children have been sacrificed on the altar of prosperity. That is when Moses' warning echoes through the hall of history: 'Then watch yourself, that you do not forget the Lord who brought you from the land of Egypt, out of the house of slavery.'"[21]

Closely related to this question is the last one I want to address in this chapter:

Question #6: What if my parents don't want me to live at home?

A: You should submit to your parents, and compromise with them if at all possible.

One of the important lessons we learn by living at home is to submit to the godly leadership of our parents. Sometimes, though, even on issues of conscience, our parents are not going to agree with our convictions. These *What if?* questions may be giving them more pause than they give us—they might not like the idea of you "sitting at home," all day, even after you have implemented some of the ministry ideas I am going to share in Part Four.

In this instance, we might have to submit to our parents in the same way that a wife submits to the husband who wants her to work outside of the home to supplement their income.

My advice to a young woman in this situation would not be to wave books like this in her mom and dad's face, or to fall into the sins of bitterness and pride when dealing with disagreements with our parents.

Instead, I would encourage you to patiently petition them. Perhaps you can take classes at a local community college or take online courses in order to honor them. Is there a job you can take as a nanny or babysitter in order to bless the homes of others if your parents want you to work outside of the home? Do you have a friend whose father has a home business that is in need of extra hands?

If your parents send you off to school, is there a local church that you can plug into? Is there a family at the church that you admire? Is there a Titus 2 woman that you can learn from?

Here are some qualities you can search for in a mentor, even if your mom is not able to be nearby:

Reverent in their behavior

Not slanderers

Or slaves to much wine

Teaching what is good.

How do we define teaching what is good? These women are able to teach us to:

Love our husbands and children

Be self-controlled

Pure

Workers at home

Kind

And submitting to their own husbands.

These qualities are straight from Titus 2:3-5. Even if we are not able to reap the benefit from them in our homes, we can search them out at our local church, or even in our reading material.

Even if you are the daughter of unbelieving parents, there are ways to honor them while still honoring the convictions that the Lord has laid on your heart. It takes creativity sometimes, and dedication, yes, but it is not impossible.

Maybe you aren't as worried about how your parents are looking at you, though, as you are about how you feel stay-at-home daughters might be eyeing you. What if you work a nine-to-five? What if you are off at college? Are you afraid that stay-at-home daughters like me are eyeing you with disdain? Are you eyeing *them* with disdain just to keep things mutual?

In the next chapter, I want to answer a common barrage of questions: "Are you judging me?"

CHAPTER FOURTEEN

Are You Judging Me?

We have talked about the *Why?* questions, the *What if?* questions . . . the hardest questions to answer are still ahead of us—those are the *Are you judging me?* questions. These are the inquiries that come from all different kinds of people, from the rabid and combative feminist to the insecure college student to every type of person in between. I get these quite a bit, and you might find that you do as well.

First, a brief word about judging—we all do it.

Webster's 1828 dictionary has a very apt definition of judging:

> *To form an opinion; to bring to issue the reasoning or deliberations of the mind.*[22]

I would argue, based on a sound definition of judging, and based on biblical commandments to rightly judge the behavior of others, as we will be judged by the same standard (Matthew 7), every time we draw an opinion on someone's actions, whether favorable or unfavorable we are making a judgment call. The important things to remember when forming an opinion, though, is to 1) align that opinion with God's Word, and 2) state that opinion with the love that God commands of us in his Word (1 John 3:11-24).

The first way to deal with "are you judging me?" questions is to learn to define *judgment* properly. We all judge—in asking that question in an accusatory tone, the questioner is judging *you*—what the question-asker really wants to know is if you think your life choices make you superior to other young women. The second way to approach "Are you judging me?" questions is to check our tone.

We certainly do not want to come across as setting ourselves up on some type of pedestal and looking down our noses at anyone who doesn't share our opinions; but we also don't want to renege when it comes to boldly proclaiming the truth of the gospel.

How can we strike that balance?

Let me offer a bit of a personal testimony: Something I have to constantly remind myself to do is to *speak the truth in love*. I tend to run off with "speak the truth" without remembering the "in love" portion of the passage (Ephesians 4:15). For someone who is often prone to sensitivity when crying over an insipid novel or a cheesy romantic comedy, I must admit, my default mode is not graciousness—it's impatience. It's something I'm working on, though, and it's easier to work on once I understand that it's a problem. I may be right, 100%, about a certain topic, but I lose credibility when my stated goal (to bring glory to God) belies my apparent state of mind (pride).

That's the first step to communicating with a spirit of humility: if you think too highly of yourself, it is sure to come across in what you're saying. However, when we keep the focus off of ourselves and on the Lord, we realize that we are but dust, only instruments to be used for God's glorious purposes. It is only because of the sacrifice of his son on the cross that we're even able to feel the convictions that we're called to speak so boldly about, not because of anything that we have done. The best way to communicate this humbling truth to others is to keep it on the forefront of our minds when we're sharing the truth of the gospel with them.

Secondly, as we communicate, we need to do so with love. Our reason for sharing the gospel with an unbeliever, or sharing a difficult truth with a fellow believer should not be to rack up cosmic brownie points, but to bring glory to God. We should speak from loving hearts, with gentleness, graciousness, and earnestness. Our purpose should not be to tear others down, but to show that, in light of the righteousness of God, *we are all sinners*—only by his grace can justification, adoption, and sanctification take place. Often, when people talk about a judgmental spirit, what they mean is an abrasive, confrontational, or condescending attitude. Our tone in any discussion should be one of equal Christian charity and firm conviction.

Which leads me to my final point, we need to speak from convictions that have been drawn from God's Word. When we know our words are supported by Scripture, we can speak them with confidence and conviction. Learn to articulate your stance on the issue at hand, so that you will be ready to answer objections and follow-up questions. As an aside here, accusations of a judgmental spirit aren't always grounded in the attitude of the speaker, but in the attitude of the hearer; sometimes, biblical conviction can be a controversial subject. When we've done all we can to state our opinions with grace and clarity, the best thing we can do when someone shows continued opposition to our words isn't to adopt a pushier attitude, but to step aside and know that it is God who changes hearts and convictions.

All of that said, I want to answer a handful of the most popular questions in this vein, in hopes of encouraging you to carefully think through your own answers to them.

Question #1: What Is Your Belief on College? Do you think that women should go to college?

A: I think all young women should carefully reevaluate the decisions that they have made based on the status quo, rather than on God's Word.

This was one of the first responses (anonymous) that I received on my blog in a post where I opened up the floor for questions. I already had an article prepared on the subject, because I knew it was coming!

Many things came into play with my decision not to take the traditional route to post-secondary education; the twofold question above was one I pondered for quite some time: 1) what did I think about college, and, as a young woman, with my aspirations; 2) would I be attending. It was an ongoing discussion between my parents and me, and I had a massive paradigm shift from, as a little girl, yearning to be an Ivy League graduate, to, as a sophomore in high school, daydreaming about becoming a UCLA or NYU graduate who made Shyamalan-esque films, to, as a junior, researching schools with a much more Christ-exalting curricula, to as a senior, deciding to do away with the typical college experience altogether.

First off, since college is a form of furthering one's education, I had to consider what the purpose of my education was. As a Christian, I believe that purpose falls in line with my ultimate purpose: to glorify God and enjoy Him forever. I wanted all levels of my education to be effective in equipping me for that calling. There were several things that made me shy away from my UCLA and NYU ideals. One was a five-point sermon my dad's been preaching to Trey and me since we entered high school:

- Most BA degrees aren't worth the paper they are written on.

- Four years is too much time to waste.

- $80,000 (room&board/state school) to $250,000 (room and board/Ivy League) is too much money to spend.

- College is not for everyone.

- Most universities are philosophically antagonistic to Christianity.[23]

American colleges today aren't what they once were, and with the amount of time and money poured into young peoples' education today, I think the results being offered are, most often, sub-par. Young men and young women would benefit from taking a long, hard look at the way post-high-school education is conducted in America, making decisions, not based on the status quo, but on how to be good stewards with the time and the gifts that the Lord has given them.

After much consideration, I decided against the traditional college route. The first two years after I graduated were spent under the tutelage of my parents, helping my mother with the household duties while working full-time for my father as his research assistant. If people asked me what I did for a living, I'd probably quip that I was the all-purpose household and office assistant/brother-wrangler/sous-chef. I was still learning (at that time, I was researching for Daddy's latest book, *What He Must Be*) from both of my parents, particularly from my mother, because I had ample time to tag along and take notes.

Towards the end of that two-year period, we found an alternative to the traditional college route that allows me to still be just as involved with my family life, and I am now enrolled in an online degree program called CollegePlus![24] I'm an English major, and am able to pursue my passion for literature and writing at home while shaping and pursuing the other passions in my life. There is no one-size-fits-all approach to education (which, as homeschoolers, is something that we definitely know). Doing college this way affords me the opportunity to continue to live at home under the protection and discipleship of both of my parents, as well as to be involved in my family life in a unique way that I believe many college-age gals are missing out on.

And, just a note here, for those who often tell me that they admire my "discipline" for being able to pursue an online college degree in lieu of being told what to do every step of the way by a traditional college. I think there is something seriously amiss in a world where students are thought responsible enough to be shipped away from their parents and make wise decisions on a secular college campus, but not responsible enough to take initiative and study under the guidance of their parents at home.

As to question number two, should Christian girls go to college? Fortunately for me, that's not my decision to make. I believe, as it occurred in our home, adult daughters should have open, honest discussion with their parents when deciding which route to take after high school. While I definitely believe that far too many Christian students go to college simply because it's "what you're supposed to do after high school," I also believe that too many Christian young women are making these choices without the guidance of their parents, apart from the authority and the wise counsel of mom and dad. For me to tell you that my word is law in this area is for me to usurp your parents' God-given authority in that area, which is something I'm definitely *not* comfortable doing. While there are no Bible verses that speak directly to the issue of college, I think a thorough study of God's Word would prove invaluable for your approach to education and home life in general.

As another aside, though, I must say that I do not equate the question of whether or not a young person decides to go to college with whether or not young people should be educated; when asked the second question, my answer is an emphatic *yes*; I simply don't believe the only or the best way for a young person to be educated is on a college campus. Depending on their chosen career paths, young men as well as young women would often do well to cut out the time-consuming, money-guzzling venture that the traditional college education is. All I want to do is to encourage young ladies to rethink their presuppositions not only regarding education, but in regards to the aspirations that your education leads you to.

However, I can share with you, as a young woman, some of the reasons I decided against going off to school. It was more important for me to remain under the protection of my father and the discipleship of my mother than it was for me to travel cross-country to sit under the discipleship of others. I believe my primary calling is towards my home, and there is no other place I'd rather be, here in my family's home for now, and, Lord bless, someday running a home of my own and educating my own children. I had no desire for a career that would take me away from that sphere. I believe that a Christian home is the best training ground that young women can be afforded, and that the safest place a young woman can be is under her parents' authority.

For too long in our culture, parents have been training their daughters in the exact same way that they train their sons, launching their female arrows to go through life the same way their male arrows do. Fathers have been abdicating their duty to protect their daughters; mothers have neglected their duty towards discipleship and guidance. Young women have not only lost their femininity, but they've lost their desire for the biblical role that the Lord has called them to. We no longer want to be wives and mothers, and we no longer realize the power of that calling. As a result, many of us no longer realize what a unique time in our lives this can be, not only to take advantage of our ministry to our home and families, but the minister to others through that sphere.

Question #2: Do you think that all young women should live at home like you?

A: I think all young women should carefully reevaluate the decisions that they have made based on the *status quo*, rather than on God's Word.

Again, this is an actual blogging question I receive quite often.

This answer is exactly identical to the last for a number of reasons. Again, I didn't grow up planning on staying home after I graduated high school. My focus has shifted. My parents are both incredibly loving and supportive individuals who have always taught us to form our own convictions (except for matters of the gospel). I know I could be off at college right now, working on the English/History double major of my former dreams (or the not-as-practical screenwriting degree), doing something completely different with my life. But this is where I am right now, because of a personal conviction that I arrived upon in God's own timing, and because I *want* to be.

You and I should not be staying home because we're out to prove anything. We should be here because we feel that it's what the Lord has called us to do. In the same way, we ought to encourage all young women to do what they believe the Lord is calling them to do. And I don't say that in the relativistic sense of the phrase ("It's all good—whatever works for you is what's right in the sight of God!"), but in the sense that the Holy Spirit has to bring the desire and conviction into your heart—blessedly, it's not my responsibility to convict you. Through a diligent search of God's Word, frank conversations with your parents, and, again, a reevaluation of the *status quo*, you should make this decision with caution.

I don't think that staying at home makes me better than girls who go off to college and, upon graduating, pursue careers outside of the home—but I do think that staying home is a valid, biblical option for young women, and it is an option that should not be dismissed because of the feministic tendencies of our society. And it's an option that young women who have the privilege of coming from stable, Christian homes would do well to consider, and daughters who are frustrated with the options the world has offered them would do well to consider. Beyond that, I love to talk to girls considering coming home, because my biggest encouragement is that if you're doing it out of drudgery, your time will be less fruitful then it is torturous—if you're kicking and screaming your way home from college, don't come. If you're doing it out of a sense of love, though, and a sense of conviction, and if it's a place where you can be productive, and if you have peace in your decision, it's so very worth it.

Question #3: What if I want to come home, but I don't have the kind of family you have?

A: Look forward to building that sort of family unit for your own daughters, and search for a stable environment to flourish until then.

I grew up in a stable Christian environment because my parents—who were not afforded that environment in their childhood—purposed to provide it for my brothers and I. They have built our lives around the Word of God, and have guided our focus towards the ultimate goal of glorifying the King of Kings. Because I know what the Lord has allowed Mama and Daddy to overcome to get to this point, I'm even more grateful for the godly legacy they're providing for me, and the legacy I'll be able to provide for my children someday, Lord willing. Are we perfect? No. But we're constantly reforming and redirecting our focus, making sure it's always on the Lord.

Multigenerational faithfulness is a blessing of a concept—but we have to realize that multigenerational faithfulness has to start *somewhere*. If not with your grandparents, it has to start with your parents. If not with your parents— it has to start with you. Because if you don't purpose to instill a legacy of faith into your children, they will come to the same place as the anonymous commenter above, and to the same place as other young women floundering for lack of a biblical home environment to flourish in.

The first step to embracing a biblical standard for family life may not be growing up in a home where your father was the loving shepherd of your family, who instilled the Word of God in you and your siblings from a young age; where your mother was your father's faithful helpmeet, who exemplified biblical womanhood for you day-by-day, through her care for your family; where you were encouraged to develop strong relationships with your siblings, to encourage them in the faith. The first step may be coming to a point— looking around at your broken home—and acknowledging that things are *not* right. That your situation—whether a floundering *status quo* or a fractured, harmful environment—is not ideal.

In doing so, we can grasp a vision that is so much bigger than the here and now. For multigenerational faithfulness to start in our future homes, we need to purpose right now to be the mothers and the wives that the

Lord has called us to be. For those of us with fractured families, this may mean being the mother to our daughters that we didn't have, or the wives to our husbands that our mothers weren't to our fathers. It may be refusing to settle for a man who cannot be the father to your children that you wanted your father to be to you.

A call for strong, biblical families doesn't just hit the ears of fathers and mothers who can exact change in their own homes. It is also heard by sons from broken families, and daughters from indifferent homes. The call can not always be enacted right away by a husband who takes it upon himself to provide servant leadership for his wife; sometimes, the call burns in the hearts of women with husbands who are afraid to take that first step of leadership. Sometimes, we can't throw ourselves into a biblical pattern; sometimes, we have to wait.

Young women who are coming at this from different family situations are in no way inferior to young women who have been protected, sheltered, and nurtured in a strong family environment. But if we don't acknowledge that a home that does not provide this environment is *not* ideal, we will never be able to begin anew and to encourage a godly legacy for our own children. Can the Lord work in less than ideal circumstances? Of course he can. He always does—even the most stable Christian homes are less than perfect. However, the Bible does have specific standards for biblical family life, and we can strive for them no matter where we come from.

Do you know an amazing family with a Titus 2 mother and a Titus 2 father? Eat as many dinners at their table as you possibly can. Do you go to a church with solid doctrine and a strong sense of community and fellowship? Plug in. Most importantly, do you know the Lord your God, who loves and provides for His people (Luke 12:22-31)? He can also provide for you as you wait patiently on his timing and leading in your life.

Question #4: What if I did search the Scriptures, but I don't agree with you? Do you still think I can be a Christian?

A: Yes.

It's just as simple as that.

Don't be afraid if someone on the outside looking in asks you what may seem like a ridiculous question; just answer it. Do you believe in the power of our risen Lord *plus* the power of a particular life style to save you? Or not? Because, in essence, that's the question, isn't it? Do I believe in the power of the Gospel to transform lives . . . only if it's lived out in everyone else's life the same way it's lived out in mine? Or do I believe in the power of the Gospel to transform lives . . . period?

Well, that's an easy question to answer; because I am a wretched sinner saved by God's incomparable grace, because any good within me is a result of his mercy and not of my own merit, because I'm constantly being molded and shaped into the image of His Son, my answer is definitely, positively the latter. My family's going through Galatians right now; having just hit chapter 3 this morning, I really couldn't give any other answer with a straight face. There are radically saved people who live radically different lives than I do. I don't have an "us against them" mentality when it comes to those different people; I strive to have a gospel-centered focus, which means rallying together on the points of God's Word where we agree, challenging each other where we disagree, but doing so always in a spirit of love. Am I passionate about my life's choices—you bet; I wouldn't have made them if I wasn't passionate about them. I wouldn't live my life so counter-culturally if I wasn't convicted about certain aspects of it.

I'm not fond of any question that starts with "Do you think someone can be a Christian if . . . " because it immediately takes the focus off of Christ and puts it directly on our works. As Christians, we should be striving to live lives that please the Lord *because we want to serve* the God that saved us, not because we think we need to live our lives a certain way *in order to be* saved. The evidence of our changed life is a love for the Lord's commandments (John 14:15).

Living out these principles may, indeed, look different from family to family. If you ever go to a church where everyone looks, sounds, and dresses exactly alike, check yourself. Are these people really following the leading of the Lord on their lives? Or are they looking for an easy answer that's going to be spoon fed to them? I definitely want to encourage the former, not the latter. It's not impossible to agree on foundational principles for Christian living, but practices vary. Even the most like-minded of us don't always agree on some of the biggest decisions (a friend of mine and I shuddered whenever we walked past the McCain/Palin bumper stickers in our church's parking lot last November, just for dramatic effect—we were die-hard third-party voters).

As we live our lives, there are going to be some things that we do differently from the other daughters around us. Our walk is going to look a bit different. Our talk is going to look a bit different. We will be blessed by the ministries of daughters who are serving the Lord in a different sphere—we may find ourselves blessing them as well. And although we may disagree with some Christian sisters we are blessed to call our friends on various aspects of some of their life choices (as they sometimes disagree with ours), Lord willing, we don't always have to break relationship over those disagreements. And because we're serving the same Savior, even if we aren't traveling the same exact journey, we can encourage each other on the points we *do* have in common (clumsiness, boy trouble, modesty hardships, political disenchantment, and a lack gracefulness and graciousness seem to be universal ills—who'd have thunk?), and, perhaps to challenge presuppositions or answer questions about the areas where we vary.

So, from one sister-in-Christ to another, don't *ever* conform for the sake of conforming, not to the world around you, or to a girl like me, who's chosen to do things a little differently (Romans 12:1-2 says it quite well). Make your decisions based on your convictions regarding the Word of God, and make His glory your aim. Then, we'll both be working towards the same goal. This take doesn't weaken the importance of following biblical precepts (Titus 2:3-5 tells us what's at stake here: "so that the Word of God may not be blasphemed"), but it does take the focus off of us and puts it right back where it always belongs: on Christ.

CHAPTER 15

Being Ready with an Answer

Learning to Answer My Own Questions

When I was growing up, I always used to joke that I hated asking my parents questions, because they *never* just gave me the easy answers! If I asked my mother what "DNA" stood for, she'd tell me to go look it up in the dictionary; if I asked my father who was "right" in the War Between the States, have gave me a stack of books to read; if I asked my mother who Sojourner Truth was, she went out and bought me a biography; when I asked my father if the bombing on Hiroshima and Nagasaki was a morally justifiable action on behalf of the United States, he asked me what I thought and why.

If I asked a question about any subject from the Adamic covenant to eschatology, Daddy usually turned the question right back around: "What do you think?" and if I had an answer, he'd ask me to back it up using examples from Scripture; and if I didn't have an answer he'd not only point me to the applicable Scriptures, but he'd also give me three or four books to read on the subject. If my mom was listening in, she might request a report on my answer to the question.

Of course, that reaction didn't *really* stop me from asking questions. In fact, it made me even more curious. One question leads to another... and another... and another. I didn't know it then, but my parents were training me, teaching me the true meaning of 1 Peter 3:15-16. They wanted me to be prepared to make a defense from God's Word.

Looking for Answers

In this instant gratification culture, it can be easy to become impatient about diligent study of the Scriptures. We want results *fast*, microwavable Christianity, add water and stir doctrine. Instead of searching the Scriptures for ourselves, many times, we turn to others for answers for *every single question*. We want them to do all of the footwork of studying the Scriptures for us, and, in return, we want a list of rules to live by derived from their understanding of God's Word.

I think that might just be the wrong approach. When we're studying Scripture, oftentimes, it's helpful to eliminate the middle man. This way, the importance and sufficiency of Scripture is our focus (2 Timothy 3:16). Because, really, that ought to be our focus, not the nerves of answering a hard question, or the fear of doubts about a certain subject. Then, our first reaction when we're asked a tough question isn't to think, "What would so-and-so say?" but it's "how would the Lord have me act?"

My parents knew this. And growing up—in the safety of my home—was the perfect place for me to search the Scriptures for myself, to learn to come to my own conclusions . . . *under the watchful guidance of my parents* (Ephesians 6:4). I'm always learning something—from my parents, from my research, from my Bible study, from family worship, from a conversation—and I'm always questioning what I've learned. I've also learned how to phrase my questions a little differently: instead of, "Daddy, is Obamacare a good thing?" it's "Daddy, I was reading *The Communist Manifesto* and came across a passage that had to do with this healthcare issue; I was searching God's Word, and needed some guidance about how to defend my position on healthcare, which is—" (Okay, so perhaps I'm not that eloquent, but I think you get the gist of it). Then, we can talk, and our conversation is fruitful.

Why is this so important?

First off, as I said, it keeps the Scripture, not man's opinions, as our priority. Secondly, it drives us back to God's Word for answers. Third, it helps us to filter the advice we *do* receive through the grid of the Scriptures, instead of the grid of popular opinion. Finally, it guards us from legalism. Instead of living our lives by a list of rules that someone else has derived for us, we're learning and seeking out the biblical principles in God's Word, and are able to defend them for ourselves. Not that we can't glean advice from others, but that advice should be secondary.

Under the guidance of our parents, trusted mentors, our elders, and with the help of all of the resources at our fingertips, we can become more adept at defending the faith for ourselves. And as we study the richness and depth of God's Word free of distraction, we will better understand the beauty of His precepts and how they apply to our lives.

Now, I want to add that, whenever my parents sent me off to find answers to my own questions, there was always a time when I came back to share my findings, and a discussion about what I'd learned. Because my father is the head of my home (Ephesians 5) and because it is the job of both of my parents to impress the law of the Lord on my heart (Deuteronomy 6), they have always guided me in my study. However, they also impressed on me the importance on being able to articulate our beliefs—*my* beliefs—for myself.

Developing a sound systematic theology takes more than punching your questions into Google or running and asking someone to do the study for you. But it's also richer to spend time in God's Word and in resources that point us back to God's Word than to count on others to offer us doctrine-in-a-box. Working through tough issues can be a difficult experience, but working through them with God's Word as our blueprint is our best bet for aligning our beliefs to the principles we find there. It also helps us to deepen our personal relationship with Him.

That's why my mom and dad almost never (and still don't usually) answered my questions without making me do some footwork first. And of course, now I understand that principle a little better than I did at twelve years old.

Standing On Your Own Two Feet

It wasn't until I grew a little older that I realized that many of my peers hadn't been taught to think the same way that I had. They wanted to be spoon-fed their answers in a way my parents never taught me to desire. Their answers for why they wanted to live at home until they graduated, why they wanted parental involvement in their romantic relationships, why they were seriously considering homeschooling their children, or any other number of convictions had always come down to a simple, "That's just how I was raised."

There are a couple of problems with this response. First, it isn't really a biblical response. Even if you have been raised "in the nurture and admonition of the Lord" (Ephesians 6:1), your parents' convictions came from his word, not simply from tradition (Deuteronomy 6). Once you become an adult, it is important to be able to own and articulate those convictions, not just because you are going to receive questions about them, but because you need assurance in your own walk with Christ.

Secondly, this answer definitely reinforces the stereotype of the sheltered, brainwashed stay-at-home daughter. "I live here because my daddy's making me." "I didn't go to college because I don't have options." "I never really learned how to think for myself."

Third, it robs us of an opportunity to engage the culture around us. One of my father's passions is cultural apologetics. Knowing what we believe and why we believe it have always been important things in our home, and were enforced in our home-education. Our parents have always believed in protecting us, but the sentiment involved in what people usually see as living a sheltered life were absent from our childhood.

A Homeschooler's Perspective

I'm sure you've heard the arguments: Our parents are afraid to send us to public school because they don't trust us to stand up against the temptations of the world; our parents are afraid to send us to public school because we'll realize that their Christian lifestyle is outdated; our parents are afraid to send us to public school because we'll learn about "the other side." Now, true enough, there are things that parents should be *very* afraid of their children learning from a public school teacher instead of from them; and, also quite true, there is an element of sheltering to homeschooling—and quite rightly so (Psalm 1; Romans 12:1,2; 2 Corinthians 6:14ff, Colossians 2:8, etc.). I contend, however, that my parents in particular aren't so intent on sheltering me as they are on *discipling* me. And that's a big difference in terms.

My mother and father, realizing that they were raising children who would grow into adults, and knowing that, if they wanted their children to grow into capable, God-fearing, intercontinental ballistic missiles that would make a huge impact on the world around us for Christ (Psalm 127), made a choice between sending us to what we like to call "government indoctrination centers" to learn about life from a secular humanist viewpoint... or discipling us at home and teaching us about the world we live in from a Christian perspective. Their goal was: 1) to establish a biblical foundation for all areas of our education; 2) to train us to use God's Word as the grid through which we processed all of the information out there, and; 3) to process that information, and to be able to articulate a biblical defense for conflicting worldviews (1

Peter 3:14-16; Matthew 21:19-21). The goal of the public school system isn't to teach children *how* to think—it's to teach them *what* to think; and what they're teaching is not the biblical paradigm.

When we graduated high school, therefore (I in 2007, and my brother this past year), we knew about evolution; we'd read Darwin's *magnum opus*! But the difference between our education and the schooling that others in our generation were receiving was that we had learned about evolution from a Christian worldview. When we graduated high school, we knew about Marxist socialism; we'd read Marx and Engels for ourselves! But the difference between our education and the schooling of others in our generation was that we had learned about socialism from a Christian worldview. We knew about homosexuality, about the myriad of issues surrounding that topic. But the difference between our education and the schooling of others in our generation was that we had learned about homosexuality from a Christian worldview. We knew about the importance of sexual purity, not because our parents ripped Song of Solomon out of our Bibles and never spoke about the subject to us, but *because* they had frank discussions with us about the beauty and the purpose of marriage. We knew about the issue of abortion, not from the kid-gloved conversation going on in the media, but from the vile Margaret Sanger herself.

From Aristotle to Freud, my parents knew that the important thing for us to come away with after graduation wasn't a warped, happy-go-lucky view of the pagan world outside our front door, or to be afraid of handling difficult issues because we'd never been exposed to contrary views, but armed with the knowledge and *the biblical foundation for that knowledge* that would sustain us as we walked through the "real world." And that phrase is the key that differentiates our education from government schooling: that biblical foundation, and the acknowledgement—in whatever subject we undertook—that the beginning of all knowledge is the fear of the Lord (Proverbs 1:7).

As an important note, there were things that we *didn't* read, not because my parents were afraid we'd jump ship if we were exposed to opposing viewpoints, but because there was a much more edifying way to garner the information my parents wanted to teach me. Thus, I took a pass on *Madame Bovary*. Also, as an aside, my parents didn't just send us to wade in secular humanist texts without discipling us every step of the way, or, without first—before the texts were even presented to us—know that we were mature enough to handle what we were learning without becoming confounded or confused. They were very discerning of our level of discernment.

It's been a joy to see some of our extended family looking on in shocked surprise as my brother and I continue to grow throughout the years. When my parents first started homeschooling me, they were warned that as soon as I turned 18, I'd be out the door, in full-fledged rebellion, because I'd been "repressed." My parents politely explained something that rang true in my life: Because they taught me biblical principles, and didn't just pound moralisms and legalisms into my life, but, instead, a passion for God's Word, and because I understand my role in God's design, the last thing I'd want to do is rebel against the authorities he's wisely placed in my life. *I am not perfect* (quite far from it, I'm afraid, which is why I felt the need to italicize and underline that statement), but this is something that I now understand, something I now consciously strive for, and something that I'm very grateful for.

For many of you who have had the grace to be raised by godly parents, it is quite amusing to hear people assume that the only reason you would choose to live the way you do is because you are unaware of other the "options" there are for us to take advantage of. On the contrary, most of us are quite aware of them; and, with full knowledge, because we are blood-bought children of God, we are not interested in them. Yes, we want to be salt of the earth, and we want the same for our children, because it's what God commands—it is part of the reason why we live in breathe—but we don't want to be desensitized to the wickedness of the world around us as we strive to do so (Matthew 5:17-20). We don't want to go into the battle as untrained soldiers, but as skillfully trained instruments in the hands of the Lord.

And the time and place to become skillfully trained is not the battleground—it's the boot-camp.

Now, I grant—freely—that homeschooling and choosing to continue my education at home in and of itself will not automatically produce God-fearing children. God's grace does that. However, I can say with conviction that I am glad for several displays of God's grace in my life. First, that he brought my parents to salvation. Second, that he commanded them to be good stewards of the children that he had given them, and to disciple them (Ephesians 6:4). Third, that my parents took that command seriously. Fourth, that because they understood the seriousness of that command, they took it upon themselves to ensure that I had a Christian education (Deuteronomy 6). Sixth, that by God's grace, I—a wretched sinner—was made whole and am now a daughter of the living God, whose hearts chief desire is now the same as my parents: to be a vessel used for God's glory, an imperfect, faltering vessel though I may be. Finally, seventh, that, now that my days of homeschooling are behind me, I can look back and see the benefits of their labor of love, and can look forward with anxious anticipation to the day when I may be able to pour my own passion and zeal for Christ into the education of my children.

Not because my zeal alone can save them—but because it's a zeal that my Lord has commanded of me.

I pray that the Lord grants you the same passion. Whether or not you were homeschooled, whether you had a diverse education or not, your years at home are an amazing time to grow in knowledge of the Lord, of the world he has created, of his redemptive plan throughout history, and of the battlefronts that we will be warring on in our generation.

What is secular humanism? How has it effected the public school system? What exactly is feminism? How long has it been around? Is there a good sort of feminism that we should embrace? What about birth control? Where did that come from? Is that something you want to embrace for your future family? How about your children's education? Are you sending them to public or private school? Why or why not? Christianity—what's all that about? What doctrines do you embrace? What sets your denomination apart from others? Are you non-denominational? Why? Do you know church history? What's so great about Christianity? How is it different from other religions? Is it a religion or a relationship?

These are just some of the questions that you can strive to answer—there are hundreds more!

The Lord Changes Hearts

These sorts of questions—and more questions about questions—can be the jump-start to gaining confidence in your convictions, and learning how to articulate them with grace and intelligence. Living at home, you are safe, you are loved, guided, discipled, and protected. Now is the time to gird ourselves for the battle ahead.

This way, when hard questions come, we will not have to stutter or scramble for one of the books we have read to help us evaluate our convictions, and we will not have to clear our throats and look over our questioner's shoulder for our parents to hurry up and rescue us. We will be able to calmly answer what it is we've been asked.

This doesn't mean our questioners will go away.

Sometimes, questioners are not asking us things to learn, but to mock and frustrate. Sometimes, "their foolish hearts are darkened" (Romans 1:21).

My favorite question in the children's catechism that we teach my brother Elijah is probably, "Who can change a sinner's heart?"

"The Holy Spirit alone." Elijah always answers (John 3:3, Romans 8:6-11, 1 Corinthians 2:9-14, 2 Thessalonians 2:13-14; Titus 3:5-6).

Those simple words always lift a huge load off of my chest when my gospel discussions don't go as far as I'd like them to, when they get shot down right out of the gate, when I give my whole speech and my listener just waves me away like an annoying gnat. It's not about me and the good feeling I get when I convert someone, is it? It's about God's glorious plan in calling his own.

This doesn't mean we stop preaching the gospel because God will do all of the work. He most certainly could, but he has called us to be the tools he uses. For, "how then will they call on him in whom they have not believed? And how are they to believe in him of whom they have never heard? And how are they to hear without someone preaching? And how are they to preach unless they are sent?" (Romans 10)

And it doesn't mean that we won't experience disappointment at the blindness of the lost, or even the blindness of other believers in certain areas of their lives. But it does mean that we can have hope that, perhaps, the Lord has used us to plant a seed that he will later water, that can grow into the glorious fruit of regeneration or sanctification, and that our words have not fallen on deaf ears.

And that's a comfort I cannot do without!

But speaking of the gospel: Where *does* that fit in to all of this home-talk anyway?

Part Four

CHAPTER SIXTEEN

The Home and the Great Commission

The other day, I received an e-mail that stated, quite simply: Hey! I was just wondering what you might say to someone who would say this: "The Bible says, 'Go into all the world to preach the gospel,' not, 'go into all your house and preach the gospel.'" I'm just wondering. =)

Hudson Taylor once said that "The Great Commission is not an option to be considered; it is a command to be obeyed."[25] As children of the Most High, we have been given a sobering command from Jesus Christ:

> Go therefore and make disciples of all nations, baptizing them in the name of the Father and of the Son and of the Holy Spirit, teaching them to observe all that I have commanded you. And behold, I am with you always, to the end of the age. —Matthew 28:19-20

If you are a young woman whose desire is to be the helper suitable of a godly, visionary man someday—if you want to raise your children in the nurture and the admonition of the Lord day by day—if you want to take primary responsibility for their education—if you are a young woman who is committed to her family's vision, who prizes her father's protection and her mother's discipleship... eventually, somewhere along the line, you're going to get the question at the beginning of this chapter, the question I receive via e-mail, comment, and verbal communication all the time:

"Where does all this 'home-talk' fit in with the Great Commission?"

The Great Commission, Though of Incredible Importance, Is not the Only Passage in the Bible

For me, whenever I receive that question, I always point out, foremost, that Matthew 28:19-20 is not the only passage in God's Word. Titus 2:3-5, Proverbs 31:10-31, Ephesians 5:22ff; 6:1-4, Deuteronomy 6, 1 Peter 3:1-6 tell us that the Christian family is to be a priority to God's people. While it is, of course, of equal importance to minister outside of our family unit, the very requirements for ministers of God's Word show us that if we haven't been faithful ministering to the families we've been given, we are not worthy of the position of elder. 1 Timothy 3:4-5 says, "He must manage his own household well, with all dignity keeping his children submissive, for if someone does not know how to manage his own household, how will he care for God's church?"

We do know that not everyone has been blessed with a family that encourages their Christian convictions, and some have had to break ties because of that (Matthew 10:34-39, Psalm 27:10), but if we belong to a family of God's people, we have been given an incredible blessing.

How Are We Defining the Home?

Here is a question I have learned (through trial and error) to ask before answering the "home-talk and the Great Commission inquiry." *How are you defining 'your home?'* As young women who are striving to exemplify biblical femininity, the home should hold a cherished place in our hearts. However, in the twenty-first century, homes have become merely places to recharge before heading out to our real lives on the outside. We work eight to twelve hours a day, or we're in school eight hours with extracurricular activities and a part-time job afterwards, we seek our entertainment outside of the home, and we seek our identity outside of our home... when I think about what the typical American idea of a home is, I understand why most people wrinkle their nose at the idea of those "poor, restless women" who, whether because they have been forced to live there or because they're too cosseted to have any ambition beyond those four drab walls or because they lack exposure to alternative lifestyles, decide to make the home their primary focus.

Imagine, though, a different sort of place: home as a hub for ministry and discipleship. Home: where children are brought up in the nurture and the admonition of the Lord, diligently trained to impact the world outside of their doors. Home: headquarters for visionary men to lead and inspire their families. Home: the domain of visionary women who desire to bless their families, their churches, and their communities. Home: a place where those who understand the critical importance of a strong, biblically-functioning family unit to the well-being of society flourish.

It sounds like a fairy-tale to some, I know, but I live in this home. It is not perfect, but it has been built on the foundational principle that home life and family life are of prime importance, and that, if we want to minister to people outside of our four walls, the most important thing we can do is learn to minister within this sphere.

What Are We Young Women to Aspire To?

I love to read 1 Timothy 5:9-10:

> *Let a widow be enrolled if she is not less than sixty years of age, having been the wife of one husband, and having a reputation for good works: if she has brought up children, has shown hospitality, has washed the feet of the saints, has cared for the afflicted, and has devoted herself to every good work.*

Now, I am certainly not an older widow, but this sixty-year-old woman is a sight to behold; in her youth, she cherished the beauty of Proverbs 31: She was the loving wife of her husband (Proverbs 31:11), and she had a reputation for good works (Proverbs 31:31). She brought up children (Proverbs 31:28), showed hospitality, ministered to the saints, and cared for the afflicted (Proverbs 31:20), and she has devoted herself to every good work. By the time she was sixty, she had a reputation as an active member of her community and a capable manager of her home.

This doesn't mean that women should *never* leave their homes. The Proverbs 31 woman had to travel to minister to others, to do business on her husband's behalf, to further his estate, and to reach out to the needy. She was a talented woman who used her gifts to bless her family (Proverbs 31:24). She wasn't afraid of hard work (Proverbs 31:17), and she was brave (Proverbs 31:21) and creative (Proverbs 22). This does not sound to me like the type of woman who could be stuck in a box!

Your Home Reaching Out to Other Homes

When we understand what the biblical home looks like, how a biblical family operates, it allows us to use the home as a springboard to reach out to others. The most obvious way I can think to do this would be to show hospitality to strangers (Hebrews 13): visiting missionaries who need a place to stay— unchurched neighbors—those in need. We use it to train up children who may set up their homes in other states or on other continents as a headquarters for ministry (Psalm 127). We use it as a place to recharge and refocus after we have been out doing ministry in the community. I am just as passionate about cultural renewal as the next person, but if that renewal doesn't start where we live, we've missed a spot.

In every new member's class for our church, my dad points out that the Great Commission was first given, the "remotest parts of the earth" were not the tribal jungles we often imagine Jesus' hearers were being sent to: the "remotest parts of the earth" from Jerusalem would be... America. Often, in our haste to advance the gospel to those people "out there," we forget the importance of ministering *right here* where we have been planted, where the gospel needs advancing as well.

The girl who says she wants to grow up and become a bush-whacking missionary to an unreached people group is lauded as a heroine, the one who wants to serve the Lord by becoming a capable wife and mother is often shrugged of in disdain.

Blessedly, it is not the world's idea of success that we are after when it comes to ministry. We want to please the Lord by having the same priorities for biblical womanhood and ministry that he has in his Word. So while "I want to marry a godly man and raise up a godly generation" may not seem as impressive as other things you could mention, it is certainly important!

The Importance of Family Reformation

Richard Baxter is one of my favorite Puritan authors—my affinity for him was passed down through my Dad, who loves his works, especially *The Reformed Pastor*. On page ninety of this book—which is full of so many other gems as well—Baxter writes to pastors:

> *We must have a special eye upon families, to see that they are well-ordered, and the duties of each relation performed. The life of religion, and the welfare and glory of both the Church and the State, depend much on family government and duty.*

> *If we suffer the neglect of this, we shall undo all. What are we like to do ourselves to the reforming of a congregation, if all the work be cast on us alone; and masters of families neglect that necessary duty of their own, by which they are bound to help us? If any good be begun by the ministry of any soul, a careless, prayerless, worldly family is like to stifle it, or very much hinder it; whereas, if you could but get the rulers of families to do their duty, to take up the work where you left it, and help it on, what abundance of good might be done! I beseech you, therefore, if you desire the reformation and welfare of your people, do all you can to promote family religion.*[26]

He goes on to say:

> *Get masters of families to do their duty, and they will not only spare you a great deal of labour, but will much further the success of your labours. If a captain can get the officers under him to do their duty, he may rule the soldiers with much less trouble, than if all lay upon his own soldiers.* **You are not likely to see any general reformation, till you procure family reformation. Some little religion there may be here and there; but while it is confined to single persons and is not promoted in families, it will not prosper, nor promise much future increase.** *(emphasis mine)*[27]

These words came from a man who lived in the seventeenth century, who had no idea what sort of state the American family would find itself in three hundred years down the road. Our sharply fragmented sense of home life greatly misses the mark when it comes to true discipleship and evangelism within the home.

What You Can Do to Help

So what can we daughters do to help?

As daughters, we are not commanded to be the spiritual leaders of our homes. This is something that has been delegated to our father, principally (Ephesians 5:22ff, 6:1-4). If our father has abdicated this role in his home, aside from respectfully petitioning him, we can make sure to carefully diagnose our own spiritual health, reading the things that will edify us and strengthen us as we grow into the women the Lord has called us to be, and pray—as we have mentioned before—that the Lord has given you a passion for family life that will bless a godly husband someday as you work alongside him to impart a multigenerational vision to your children.

If your father *is* a believer, though, and a discipler of his family, the best thing you can do to promote spiritual unity in your home is to *get onboard*. Show interest in your father's plans for your family. Buy him edifying books for his birthdays. Read edifying books yourself, and share your own thoughts and revelations with him. Cultivate a biblical relationship with both parents, sharing your heart with them on Scriptural matters, and seeking their advice for important issues in your life, trusting that they will use God's Word as their compass.

Even if your parents are "weaker" believers than you are—if you were saved first, or if you have more conviction in certain areas than they do— honor them by praying to the Lord for their spiritual growth, and letting them know that they are in your prayers. Instead of puffing up in a spirit of pride, model honor and submission before them, and encourage them as they grow in grace. Even if your dad is new to leading your family in family worship, for instance, do not laugh at any awkwardness he shows, or snicker when he trips over his words or become frustrated because you think "other dads" could do things better. The Lord gave you the father that you have or a purpose, and that man is precious in God's sight, especially when he is striving to carry out the Lord's commands before his family.

But What is Multigenerational Faithfulness?

Multigenerational faithfulness starts with the legacy that your parents are instilling in you—it carries on when you instill that legacy in your own children—and, by God's grace, it can advance as your children and children's children follow suit.

Multigenerational faithfulness is not some kind of assurance that your children and grandchildren will follow the commands of Christ perfectly. It is not insurance against unregenerate relations or rebellion. But as we read passages like Deuteronomy 6, we see that imparting a godly legacy will be part of our job description as parents, not in pursuit of perfection, but in pursuit of obedience to the Most High:

> *Hear, O Israel: The Lord our God, the Lord is one. You shall love the Lord your God with all your heart and with all your soul and with all your might. And these words that I command you today shall be on your heart. You shall teach them diligently to your children, and shall talk of them when you sit in your house, and when you walk by the way, and when you lie down, and when you rise. You shall bind them as a sign on your hand, and they shall be frontlets between your eyes. You shall write*

them on the doorposts of your house and your gates.
—Deuteronomy 6:4-9

This sounds a lot like Paul's admonition for father's to raise their children in the nurture and admonition of the Lord, doesn't it (Ephesians 6:1-4)?

By submitting to our parents—by seeking to serve them and to aid them as they serve others for God's glory—and by hearkening to their word in our lives, we are promoting unity within our homes. And that's a good thing!

But I'm Not a Parent Yet!

Even though we are unmarried daughters living at home, nevertheless, we still have a responsibility to submit ourselves to the spiritual leadership of our parents and to the sanctifying influence of the Holy Spirit as we grow in grace.

Read that passage Deuteronomy 6 again, very carefully. Do you notice phrases like "you shall love the Lord your God with all your heart and with all your soul and with all your might" and "these words that I command you shall be on your heart" come *before* "you shall teach them diligently to your children?" Before we can become the godly mothers who will inundate their children with sound doctrine, we must be mothers who are able to live as examples of faith as we walk alongside them. This does not start the first time we want to admonish them—it doesn't start the first time we hold them in our arms—it doesn't start when we say "I do" to a godly man—it starts right now, while we are still growing and changing and being challenged in our youth.

The Lord is gracious—he can aid and equip parents who did not even hear the gospel until they were adults—like my dad. However, as we *have* heard the gospel, and as we do claim to belong to Christ, we have a responsibility to take his calling on our lives seriously.

So What about Unreached People Groups?

This does not mean a family will never minister to those in another country. But my idea of a missionary is someone who plants their life among the people they want to minister to: They set up their home, bring or start their family there, and set in for the long haul among those to whom they have been called to preach the gospel. We know families that have done this very thing in places from Spain, Germany, Mexico, and other countries. In fact, the man who first shared the gospel with my dad was so committed to serving in Mexico and so immersed his family in the culture and community there that both of his formerly American daughters speak accented English. The Christian household—wherever it is planted—is a vital springboard for ministry. This is not to say that there is no place for single missionaries, but the importance of a household is often overlooked in our modern day and age.

So What about Single Young Women Who Want to Be Missionaries?

To answer this question, I've got to start with my understanding of missions work. In the Great Commission, we are commanded to go forth and make disciples of all nations. As we read the NT, we see that this is done, principally, through the unapologetic proclamation of the Gospel, but also planting of healthy churches.

I take issue with young women traipsing off to the mission field less because of my beliefs about womanhood than because of my belief about disciple-making. Long-term missions are far more effective than short-term, and church-planting (from my perspective) is the work of men. When entire families plant their lives on foreign soil, they minister to foreign communities in a whole new way. They impact entire families instead of just individuals. They change the tide of the culture instead of a few people. They perform hospitality and show people what Christian family life—what a Christian culture—looks like.

Our family maps out its hospitality days for the month: half for our church family and friends, the other half for our unchurched neighbors. I don't buy that you have to make a profession of ministry to make an impact: Families across generations and around the world have been impacting society since the days of the early church, ministering to orphans and widows through hospitality and hands-on ministry. I just don't happen to believe that the only way to be effective way for young women to minister to the widows and the orphans is to journey forth unprotected (James 1:27).

Ministry in and through the home is simple. The Bible has given a clear directive for that as well: hospitality (Romans 12:13, 1 Timothy 5:10, Hebrews 13:2, 1 Peter 4:9). Mothers without children have opportunities to invite families into their homes several times a week to get to know them and to minister to them; they can volunteer at their local crisis pregnancy center, counseling other women; they can help other women in their church who have children and may need a break; they can go out and witness to the sick and aid the elderly. Wives of missionaries across the world can do the same for unreached people groups. I have seen this happen, and it is a beautiful thing.

If we are not serving the Lord on His terms, we're serving ourselves, and we're letting the world define service to him, not His Word.

Someday, I may be able to visit my good family friends in Dubai, ministering alongside a strong man and his wife and helping with their children for a time, working as my father's ambassador overseas and helping to bless another family while I'm there. Someday, I may advise another young lady to minister overseas short term with another family unit who is established in overseas mission work? But, I see no biblical precedent for a young lady ministering overseas as an independent entity, unprotected and, to a larger degree, inefficient in bringing about the huge cultural change we're after. Families make that change; it's not as popular a notion, but by God's grace, I think it's spreading.

But What about Missionaries like Amy Carmichael, Gladys Alward, & Mary Slessor?

I know a lot about these women. They were all heroes of mine growing up! Our library holds each and every one of their biographies. They served the Lord in mighty ways, and poured out their lives for him on foreign soil. My opinion of women missionaries in no way invalidates the sacrifices that they made, or that those sacrifices did, indeed, bear great fruit.

However, I am not a pragmatist—just because a Christian has done something that bears fruit, does not mean that there is biblical provision for that action. When I approach the question about the biblical validity of a female missionary, I try to approach it from a biblical perspective, not necessarily a historical perspective, because even God's people are prone to misunderstanding his precepts.

These women were brave. They were incredibly virtuous, and they loved the Lord with all of their hearts. But this does not mean that they were above ignorance of the Lord's precepts, or above correction. We will never know if the same work could have been done by different people in different ways at different times, because the Lord ordained to use them, even if they were misguided.

We have to be so careful when speaking about women like these, because their sacrifice is going to be an emotionally charged subject. However, before you set your heart on becoming the next Amy Carmichael, please consider how the Lord might use you right here and now for his glory.

The Bigger Picture

My family has had the unique opportunity of traveling all over the world as my father preaches the Gospel, even living overseas for a year. My brother Trey alone has been to Zambia, South Africa, Germany, Northern Ireland, Romania, and several other countries to minister to others. The countries we have traveled to have been extremely diverse, but everywhere we go, we can be sure of one thing: We're going to find families. Part of making disciples of the nations is teaching them "to observe all that [Jesus] ha[s] commanded [us]." That includes a biblical vision for the home. And a truly biblical home's influence reaches out beyond its walls to the culture around it, with the godly women who understand the beauty of a homeward calling on the front lines.

We'll talk a little more about the "how's" of this type of ministry in the following chapters.

CHAPTER SEVENTEEN

Getting Your House in Order

It may seem a little odd to start a section about reaching out to the community with getting our homes in order, but I think it's fitting, given the fact that, in the last chapter, we talked about how the home can be a springboard for ministry outside of the home. In order to effectively balance our responsibilities towards home and the responsibilities that call us outside of the home, we need to start by getting our houses in order.

What Are My Responsibilities Toward My Home?

At their core, those responsibilities include what is delegated to you, usually primarily by your mother, and secondarily by your father. This could include anything from daily chores like making your bed, sweeping the kitchen floor, and walking the dog to doing research for your dad, filing his paperwork, or helping him run his home business. A daughter's level of responsibility is going to look different from house to house, depending on what your dad does for a living, how many siblings you have at home, and how your mother likes to keep your house.

How Do I Manage My Time at Home?

This might be one of the most popular questions I get from adult daughters who live at home. It's also a question that's almost impossible for me to answer. Because every home is different, and because every young woman is going to have a different set of responsibilities from home to home, time management is not something that I can lay out, blow-by-blow, in a book. Part of finding the joy in living at home is setting your own pace.

However, it might be helpful if I share my daily schedule (which is subject to change, depending on what time of year it is):

My day usually starts before dawn. My dad and I are both early risers, two-of-a-kind, who only need five hours of sleep to function. Even if I've had a late night, I still try to be up before anyone else in the house, because I enjoy the quiet of the early morning, and walking out of my bedroom with a number of chores for the day already marked off my list. I hear my talent for surviving on five hours of sleep will dissipate the more children I have, but, for now, I'm enjoying it.

While the house is still dark, and my mind is at its sharpest, right after my quiet time, I set to my college studies. At this writing, I'm a junior in an online college program—my schedule varies, from sometimes taking a CLEP test every week or two, to taking one every month or so, depending on the subject. In a few months, my credits will be transferred to a fully accredited college, and I will start taking online courses. If I have any time left over after my studying (if it's a subject like technical writing, I usually have time left—if it's something horrific like College Algebra or Biology, I might spend all two-and-a-half hours of my morning time with my nose to the grindstone), I write. My family's day starts officially at 8:30, when I head downstairs to greet Mama, Daddy, and my oldest younger brother, Trey. We divide and conquer when it comes to getting the younger boys ready for the day, feeding the baby, and fixing breakfast.

From there, we hit the ground running. Mama is the type of woman who seems to have boundless energy. You will rarely find her sitting down for a breather, even when she needs one. I have to rush to keep up with her, helping her around the house, making meal plans together, dividing the cooking between the two of us and Daddy (who is a gourmet chef in his own right), and dividing the laundry between us (and there is a *lot* of laundry at our house, especially with our cloth diapers).

While Mama homeschools Elijah, Trey and I take care of Judah, Asher, and Baby Micah. Halfway through Elijah's lesson, I start teaching Asher. As you can imagine, since he's only three—his lesson plan is far less taxing than his penchant for hyper-activity. But he's cute as a button.

In my spare time, I love to read and write. I also work for my dad, so whenever he's working on something new or charting unfamiliar territory, I have a stack of books to keep me happy (for example, last summer, I was inundated with research regarding the homosexual community—the summer before that, we were entrenched in economics), and some web-searching for online resources as well. When things get down to the wire, I might read three to five books a week. Otherwise, though, with everything else that's on my plate, I average three to five books a month, a combination of research, studies, and leisure (currently J.I. Packer, a technical writing handbook, and Marilynne Peterson).

Now, that is by no means an exhaustive daily schedule, and it is always subject to change (month-to-month—week-to-week—maybe day-to-day!) but I hope that gives you an idea of how a home can work.

So What Would That Look Like for Me?

Although I cannot give you a detailed account of what your day ought to look like, there are some principles that my time at home is teaching me to live by:

SET A SCHEDULE

The best time management tip I was ever given came from my mother: Set a schedule.

From the time we were in primary school, Mama mapped out our chore lists on colorful pieces of paper so that we could stick a star next to each completed chore. She put our school schedules on a nice little timeframe so that we could pull out our school binders and turn to the front page whenever we wondered if we ought to be doing math or science. We even had a weekly list of virtues to work on (one week's lesson would be humility—another, selflessness). Part of my mother's penchant for planning comes from her personality. She is much more detail-oriented and diligent than I am. However, she did pass on one facet of her organizational skills on to me (I'm still working on the "keeping my bedroom clean" part), and that is understanding the beauty of a daily schedule.

Your schedule can set the pace of the day ahead, outlining important tasks you want to get done, helping you to prioritize your household responsibilities, studies, and personal projects, and allowing you to glean everything you can from your day, rather than aimlessly wandering around your house until evening time, and then wondering where all of your day has gone. A schedule can aid you in sucking the productivity out of every day.

Talk to your parents about their daily expectations of you. Map out days of the week that you have scheduled outings like piano lessons or play dates.

Write in study time. Jot down slots for projects. Discipline yourself to get up at a certain time every morning.

When we read Proverbs 31:10-31, we see that a godly woman is a woman who had the time and energy to minister in a number of amazing ways. If you had been able to follow her around for an entire day, I am sure you would have seen incredible drive and self-discipline in her character.

GAIN SELF-DISCIPLINE

A schedule will do you little good if you don't have the self-discipline to keep one. As daughters who live at home, we cannot expect our parents to have the time to micromanage us, or to help us put a neat row of checkmarks next to the items on our daily schedules. If we wish to grow into competent young women, we must prove ourselves competent in the little things—keeping a daily schedule is a start.

A great way to stay motivated is to remember the stereotype of a stay-at-home daughter: A spoiled little princess who sits on her chaise all day, eating bonbons and talking a good game about cultural reformation whilst idly reading romance novels and waiting for Prince Charming to break through the sheltered bubble of her existence and whisk her off to yonder tower.

If that isn't enough to get you running in the opposite direction, think on an even more pressing reason to be productive. The Lord has given us the days at hand to do work for his Kingdom. We are frittering away precious hours in his service when we "eat the bread of idleness."

LEARN TO BE FLEXIBLE

Still, a daily plan is just that—a plan. When a baby is born, or when a family moves, when a church is planted, when a relative dies, when someone gets married, or in any other event that disrupts the daily flow of life occurs, don't wail in despair that your schedule has been overturned. Instead, rejoice that you are in a position to lay down what you're doing and to live life alongside your family.

For me, two years ago, this included the day-to-day school aside for a trip to Northern Ireland. While that might sound heavenly to someone else, for a girl who does not like travel (particularly international) and had been telling anyone who'd listened that she wasn't a "big fan" of Great Britain since she'd lived there once upon a time, it was a sacrifice. I made it, though, because Daddy had a speaking engagement, and because at least we'd all be together.

It was a wonderful time. I fell in love with the rolling hills of Ireland. I had a sweet time with my family and made some amazing memories. And to think, I hadn't even wanted to go!

It was worth getting frisked by two burly Irish women at airport security on the way home. That's just how much fun I had.

But What Should Be on My Schedule?

I was e-mailing a sweet friend of mine a while ago, and asked her what she had been up to since we last corresponded. The list she gave sent put a huge smile on my face:

Well, I'm working on editing a book, finishing a book illustration, helping my sister sew a formal gown for a contest with a $50,000 prize, designing four patterns with five variations of each for a Project Runway contest, finishing a picture I'm drawing as a wedding gift, remodeling the house my family hopes to move into soon, cooking up ideas for the online stores my sisters and I run, starting a book of my own, and getting ready to begin reading [insert intimidating theological title here] because I just finished [insert the names of two even more intimidating titles here]. I also go out and visit the sick and elderly in our neighborhood whenever I get the chance, I'm helping with my younger siblings, I'm trying to help my family build up our farm, I help my mother with medical research that helps our community, and I also make my own make up and try to find other ways to save my father money. How about you?

How *about* me?

My list is not nearly as intimidating. At this point, I can't sew a stitch, so that would be the most glaring difference. I am not insinuating that your list has to look exactly like my friend's; on the contrary, since we all have different gifts and priorities, our lists will look incredibly different. However, I hope you see the point here: My friend lives on a farm with a host of household responsibilities, but because her dad does not have a home business that she can help with, or younger siblings to tend to, she has incredible freedom to explore her God-given gifts, talents, and abilities outside of the structured collegiate setting.

But Where Do I Start?

That list might have you shaking in your boots right about now, but, again, creating a schedule and setting goals for ourselves starts with evaluating our gifts and interests in light of our time and focus.

A good place to start would be with homemaking. For instance, I am not the world's most confident chef. Far from it, in fact. Although, for my dad, cooking is a therapeutic art, and, for Mama, certain fallback dishes are simply second nature, I'm known to get nervous at the prospect of even frying an egg.

If you are nervous in the kitchen like I am, project number one could be to become more confident at the skill. Take over one or two meals every day. Chart out meal plans. Make grocery lists. Then, practice.

The week of my dad's thirty-eighth birthday, I decided, instead of going through the stress of trying to pick a gift for him (some of us have that infamous parent who always shrugs and says, "Whatever you get me will be fine," so you know what I'm talking about here), I would use one of our new cookbooks and make him something special every night for dinner the week of his birthday.

I was incredibly insecure about the undertaking, so I picked out a Rachael Ray cookbook that was geared towards teaching kids how to cook. I started out with the preschooler-friendly recipes and made my way up. My mom wisely left me to my own devices, allowing me to make my own mistakes, and to make a huge mess of the kitchen.

And, guess what? I survived!

Maybe you're very confident in the kitchen—maybe what you need to work on is organizational skills. I'm your girl again. It is my ingrained tendency to be a pack rat—I want to keep *everything*—my first valentine, a ticket stub from my first ballet, a ticket to one of my favorite films . . . everything! However, even though neatness is not my default position, organizational projects are a huge help, from cleaning out my junk drawer(s) to organizing all of the books in my hope chest.

Start at home, and start with little things, and work your way out from there.

Moving on to Bigger Things

Academia is such a big subject when it comes to stay-at-home daughterhood. Even if you are taking courses at a local community college or getting a degree online, because you aren't going *off* to school, there are always going to be those that question whether or not you are receiving the same level of education that your college-bound counterparts are receiving.

College debate aside, there is a need in this day and age for well-educated, articulate young women who are learning about the world we live in from a biblical perspective. These years at home are a vital time for that learning and growing to take place. Part of your schedule should include stretching your mind.

This can start with something as simple as a reading list. Start by dividing your interests into subjects like theology, history, economics, politics, and homemaking. Then, talk to your parents and adults in your church about valuable books that would fit into each category—research trusted online resources to compile your list of books.

For instance, to compile your category on theology, you might start with a list that looks something like this:

- Church history: How much do I know? Where did the early church start? How was our Bible compiled? What was the Protestant Reformation? How did it differ from the Catholic tradition that came before it? What is Reformed theology? Who were our church fathers, and what did they teach?

- Doctrine: Does my family go to a denominational church or a non-denominational church? What is the difference between denominations? Do the members of my church sign a covenant? What does ours say? Does my denomination have a confession of faith? What is that confession? Where can I read more about those beliefs?

- History: What is an area of history that I am interested in? Is there a topic that I feel I need to learn more about? Buy a book that gives a survey of U.S. History or World History and highlight the areas with which you would like to become more familiar. Do you have an opinion on the atomic bomb drop of 1945? Do you know how Alexander the Great learned his title? Do you know anything about the founding of our country besides the fact that "Columbus sailed the ocean blue in 1492?"

- Politics: Turn on the local news—can you understand what the newscasters are talking about? True enough, politicians do often talk in confusing circles, but I have found it extremely helpful to start with American government circa 1776 and move forward, studying legislation and reactions to that legislation as the years went on, to fully grasp what's happening today. As Ecclesiastes 1:9 says, there is nothing new under the sun—many of the issues we're struggling with in the political arena today had their beginning in the debates of the past.

- Economics: Closely related to the last subject, pick up a book on basic economics (start with Adam Smith and move on from there) and pick up God's Word to see how much he has to say on the topic: you might just be surprised. What is socialism? What is real charity? How have different economic systems worked throughout the ages and throughout the world?

- Homemaking: Finally, homemaking books, which could include anything from a good cookbook to a book about home decorating to a book about plumbing. Any book that will help you better manage a home would fit into this category.

Bringing Ministry Opportunities into Your Home

So many of us young ladies balance not only our household responsibilities or individual studies, but also, ways that we can bring money into our homes.

The Proverbs 31 Woman is not a stranger to bringing revenue into her home (Proverbs 31:14, 24). She was as creative about it as she was industrious. Another popular question I receive regarding stay-at-home daughterhood is, "How will I make money if I don't go out and get a job?" My reply: That's really not my question to answer.

Whether your father can make you an official employee in his home business, your parents can give you an allowance if they are able, you can nanny for a family friend, you can teach music lessons from your home, you can get a part-time job working for another family in your church who has a business that you can participate in, you can start your own home business—be creative!

As you fit these business ventures—whether you're using your interest in photography to take portraits, using your knack for sewing to make clothing, or using your enjoyment for crocheting to make adorable gifts—into your daily schedule, keep in mind that your responsibilities towards your family should be a priority.

CHAPTER EIGHTEEN

To Be Hospitable

What do you think of when you hear the word *hospitality*? Do you think about a roomful of adults with tinkling glasses, laughing uproariously over stale jokes and superficial conversation? Do you think about a stodgy Victorian table set with a four-course feast, with others assembled around the table in fine raiment, afraid to spill on the white tablecloth? Or do you imagine others in *your* home, at your dinner table, looking at each other awkwardly, hoping that someone will start a conversation?

Here's what I think of: two huge pots of chili on our stove—enough people gathered around our island to make a full circle around it when we grab hands to pray—moving to grab the Styrofoam dishes from the counter so we can move through buffet-style—laughing while the younger set gives the dining room chairs to the adults and sits where they can find room—blue jeans, tee-shirts, bare feet—and did I mention *lots* of laughter?

Our entertainment is not often this casual, but my favorite way to practice hospitality is definitely with Styrofoam and giggles, new friends and old ones, and a constant flow of edifying conversation.

One of the most obvious ways that young women can use a homeward focus to minister to others is through *hospitality*. We can invite members of our church, neighbors, and out of town guests into our homes for a meal, for an overnight stay, for an impromptu party. Hospitality isn't just a convenient way to minister to others, though—it's also a command (Romans 12:13, Hebrews 13:2, 1 Peter 4:9).

But I'm Not Really Great in Social Settings

One argument that I have heard from young women who are not comfortable with the idea of hospitality is that they just aren't social butterflies! They aren't good at entertaining people!

I am what most people would consider a gregarious, outgoing person. In social settings, I tend to be the one who is trying to get a conversation rolling—I crack jokes to lighten the mood, I put myself out there instead of asking probing or uncomfortable questions—I initiate conversation with complete strangers about their shoes.

What most people don't realize about me is that I get extremely nervous in social settings. I stuff sweaty hands in my pockets—I smile a little tighter than normal—I pick at my food instead of eating a hearty meal when I'm socializing.

Because both of my parents are introverts, my brother Trey and I seem incredibly extroverted by comparison, but not until recently did I realize that I am more comfortable at home than abroad—that I have a tendency to be more wrapped up in my own thoughts and inner-workings than curious about the business of others—that, if left to my own devices, I would cling to a single friend at church on Sunday before branching out to talk to others.

However, because my parents always encouraged me to move out of my comfort zone and get others talking and thinking, I now have a natural tendency to try to get others to open up. I still get uncomfortably hot whenever I have to talk to new people—I throw half of my lunch at the church's fellowship meal in the trash (not good stewardship, I know... I try not to fill my plate, I promise), and I hope that people chalk up my extremely large smile and incessant joke-cracking to an excitement to be out of braces after two tough adolescent years and a naturally jovial temperament.

A benchmark of true hospitality is Christian love. Even if you are not a social or outgoing person, if you are a Christian, who has been commanded to show selfless love to your brothers and sisters in Christ (1 Corinthians 13), as well as to let your light shine before unbelievers (2 Corinthians 3:15-16).

Sometimes, this means stepping outside of your comfort zone and opening your home and your heart to others.

But My Home Isn't Nice or Clean Enough!

Hospitality consists of offering what we have to others—even when we fear "what we have" might not be good enough. The most important aspect of hospitality isn't having a nice home (although a clean, well-kept home is a blessing to all who enter), or being able to present your guests with the nicest things possible (the nicest of what *you* have is quite nice enough): it's about humble ministry and service for the cause of Christ.

One of my favorite instances of hospitality happened during one of those Texas hurricanes I mentioned, with that one-of-a-kind friend I told you about, who always guides me back to God's Word and puts a smile on my face. She and her family live on ten acres of land out in Conroe, and *always* have people over, from out-of-town family and friends (and sometimes strangers) to church members coming to have more fellowship after our Sunday meal is over. They are easily the most genuinely hospitable people I know.

My mom, younger brothers, and I relied heavily on their hospitality a couple of years ago when Hurricane Ike roared through Houston. Daddy and Trey were on an out-of-town trip and couldn't get back. The rest of us decided to head out to Conroe to bunker down with our friends. We all slept in the living room the night of the hurricane, spread out on the floor, on two couches, and in an easy chair. Half of us spent the next day in our pajamas, using a lighter and the gas stove to eat Ramen noodles and a pink Minnie Mouse radio with a makeshift antennae made from a wire hanger to get news about the storm. Once it passed, we all got into the car and rode out to stock up on comfort food that we ate while using some of the generator's power to watch a movie.

Now, my friends would not appreciate it if I didn't tell you that they usually make us a nice, home-cooked dinner and dress in day-clothes instead of pajamas to entertain us, but my favorite hospitable moment wasn't dancing in their car port or playing tag in their expansive backyard, or walking up and down their winding driveway having a heart-to-heart with my friend—it was closing my eyes on their living room floor and knowing that I was safe from the storm with sweet friends nearby.

You will find that most people are not as critical of you as you are of yourself. There is always a home bigger and more beautiful than yours—but, through Christ, there can be no hearts more open to others than yours!

What If They Don't Like Me?

Hospitality doesn't always happen in an organized way—it can happen as spontaneously as always having our home open to others. Authors Pat Ennis and Lisa Tatlock use Cherie Land as an example when answering the question, "How have you used your home as a center for evangelism?" in their book, *Practicing Hospitality:*

> *When we moved into our new house, I asked the Lord to show me what he wanted me to do in this neighborhood. Well, one day the neighbor lady came and asked what I did to get my children to turn out the way they did, and I said it is only by the grace of God that my children are the way they are. She wanted to help her four-year-old. A few days later, she called and said she needed to talk; she came over and was in tears, so I just shared with her and prayed for her right on the spot. I also had your first book (Becoming a Woman Who Pleases God) and had only read the first chapter and half of the second, but I gave it to her and the man that she is living with. All this took place on a day I had scheduled down to the last minute and needed to get things done. Even though I got behind because of the neighbor I was still able to get everything done. Since this has happened I purchased another copy of your book.[28]*

These beautiful opportunities for ministry may catch us completely unawares, but a heart that is completely open to the Lord's vision for hospitality should not let them pass by!

We have a lovely, older Italian couple that lives in our neighborhood. One day, shortly after they moved in, I heard a loud blast of music coming from their front yard—standing on my bed, peeling back my curtain, I could see the husband in the front yard shimmying to polka music, his wife clapping and egging him on in her terrycloth robe, him wearing knee-high socks, flip-flops, and night clothes.

I was highly amused, and even more thrilled when we had them over for dinner shortly thereafter, and when they invited us to sample their (*glorious!*) Italian cuisine, and all the days since, when that sweet lady stops by every so often with a sample of a delicious dish she's made, or a bit of news to share with us.

Practical Steps to Hospitality

Wesbter's 1828 dictionary describes hospitality as "the act or practice of receiving and entertaining strangers or guests without reward, or with kind and generous liberality."[29]

If that sounds a little simple, it's because, in a sense, it is. Hospitality simply means opening your home to guests, whether you are being met with the surprise of a neighbor dropping by, or planning for weeks in advance to host a visiting family. Opening your home to guests is one of the most obvious ways to advance the gospel, and yet, so often, we undervalue the benefits of such a ministry. Here are some simple things that have helped me to become more comfortable with the idea of being hospitable over the years:

BE PURPOSEFUL

Sometimes, it can be the hardest thing in the world to introduce yourself to someone new.

It is so much easier to sit back and wait for opportunities to come to you, isn't it? When you first walk into a new church, you're hoping that there will be a nice girl around your age standing behind the welcome table—when you meet a new friend, you're hoping that she will be very talkative and relatable so that you won't have to think up new topics of conversation.

In the dramatic world of teenage girls, something as simple as turning around in the church lunch line to shake the hand of the person behind you, offering a genuine smile as you introduce yourselves and wait to hear their name in turn is one of the most petrifying experiences that you can imagine!

Hospitality can be like that. We want to be invited over. We want to be reached out to. We want someone else to initiate, because reciprocating is so much easier than branching out first.

Sometimes, opportunities to show hospitality are going to fall right into our laps. Our pastor may ask us to open our home to a missionary family, for instance, or one of our neighbors might randomly drop by. More often than not, though, if we want to learn to be hospitable, we have to *initiate* when it comes to finding opportunities to practice.

Is there a new girl at church who you would like to get to know better? Talk to your parents about having her family over for dinner—mention the possibility of having her over for an afternoon. Are you new at church? Maybe a good way to get to know the young ladies in your fellowship would be to invite a handful of them over to spend time with one another.

BE YOURSELF

About a year ago, a young lady from our church was kind enough to invite me to her graduation tea. It was a lovely event—all of us girls dressed up, and we were served cute little finger snacks and tea or coffee from china dishes. The theme was to bring a gift for my friend's hope-chest, so presents ran the gamut from aprons to linens to cookbooks.

In the midst of the festivities, one of my friends asked me why I hadn't had a party when I graduated two years prior. A friend who knew me a little better laughed in the background. "Jasmine's not really the tea-having kind of girl."

Well, that's true—I'm not—and that's okay!

When I visit with certain friends, I know that I need to put on my prettiest frock or be prepared to have a blast as we reenact scenes from *The Importance of Being Earnest*. With others, I know that we'll pop in a familiar movie and repeat every line as the film plays on. If you come over my house, we'll probably go for a long walk and have a nice chat about anything from Jane Austen to The New Deal.

If I tried to throw an exquisite tea, I would be at a complete loss. The beautiful thing about hospitality is that you don't have to be anyone but yourself—when people come to your home, they want to get to know *your* family. You have a unique flavor and a special way of doing things. Your guest will most appreciate genuine acts of service from a heart full of Christian love: As long as you can offer these things, you are fulfilling the essence of the biblical command to *be hospitable.*

BE RELAXED

Have you ever stood on the threshold of a new friend's home, a casserole dish in hand, a long night of fellowship ahead of you—knees knocking, palms sweaty, throat dry?

I know I have. Sometimes, if I know I'm going to be having dinner with a new family next week, I'll spend the days leading up to the get-together rehearsing what subjects we can talk about, the things that we can do while we're together, and silly mistakes that I must avoid at all costs.

When you have a new friend over, and you are on the other side of that doorway, the best thing you can do to calm her nerves—and yours—is to relax. And while that's easier said than done, I don't know of any relaxation technique quite as helpful in social situations as thinking less about your nerves and your needs and your comfort zone and more about how to bless others. The anxiety seems to lift without your notice when your heart is set on blessing your brothers and sisters in Christ more-so than the number of pterodactyls that might be winging in your stomach.

BE RELATIONAL

As I will point out in the next chapter, one thing that can make carrying on a conversation with a guest difficult is our penchant to be more comfortable talking about ourselves than we are seeking to know and to serve our brothers and sisters in the Lord. One of the hardest parts of hospitality can be learning how to engage your guests in meaningful conversation. The first step to conversing well is not learning how to talk better: it's learning how to listen!

PLAN AHEAD

How many friends are you going to have over at a time? Where will they sit? What will you cook? How much food do you need? What will you do after dinner? What are some subjects that you can talk about?

One way to eliminate the awkwardness of spending time around new people is to be prepared. With some people, being prepared is going to be easier than with others: A family you see every Sunday with church is going to be a bit more familiar to you than the family your dad invites through his friend at work—the family you are meeting for the first time who will be staying with you for a weekend church conference is going to be less familiar to you than the young lady you run into whenever you go to your local junior college to take a class. However, even if you don't know much about your guests, use what you do know to be a blessing to them!

LEARN TO BE SPONTANEOUS

Still, even when you plan ahead, there are still going to be surprises sometimes. Sometimes one of our neighbors will drop in spur-of-the-moment—other times, friends may come to stay with us on short notice—sometimes, you will run out of food—sometimes, there won't be quite enough chairs. When these things happen, learn how to take a deep breath and move forward. Remember, the most important aspect is not that everything works out perfectly, that your food is going to taste better than the next house your guests are going to visit, but ministering to others "without reward, or with kind and generous liberality."

Hospitality as a Gateway for Ministry

Who are you going to have over your home this week?

What conversations will you have with them?

How will you minister to their needs?

How will you deepen your relationship with brothers and sisters in Christ?

How will you minister to unbelievers?

It can be so easy for us to grasp a vision for multigenerational faithfulness and forget how important it is that our ministry extends past the realm of our home and into the culture around us. One of the most obvious ways that this can be done is through the ministry of the home.

There are, of course, other ministries that we young ladies can take advantage of: We can help out an expectant mother from our neighborhood, or at our church—we can volunteer at the local crisis pregnancy center or soup kitchen—some of the families in our church have had the amazing opportunity of traveling to foreign countries to aid with ministries that have been set up overseas (my dad took quite a large team with him last year when he went to speak at a Reformed pastor's conference in Zambia).

Although these other opportunities can become a regular part of our everyday lives, and although they can be so important to the body of believers, and for our ministry to the unbelievers that the Lord puts us in contact with, there will be no ministry that we can engage in on as consistent a basis as hospitality. Aside from that, of all of the ministries mentioned, it is the one that is *commanded* of us.

Go ye therefore . . . and open your homes!

And, as you open them, be encouraged to hold a special place open for your sisters in the faith, who can offer encouragement along the way.

CHAPTER NINETEEN

Loving Our Sisters in Christ

Have you ever had a really horrible day? Not the mildly annoying day or the slightly stressful day, but the I-wish-I-was-ten-years-younger-and-didn't-have-to-deal-with-grown-up-problems kind of day?

I have. Unfortunately, when you're a card-carrying drama queen like I am, those days seem to happen a bit more frequently for you than for others. Nevertheless, on *some* level—even the not-so-dramatic level—I'm sure you can relate.

Those days, even after you've talked to your parents until you're blue in the face, and prayed and searched God's Word for comfort, the Lord can afford you an extra measure of comfort through a nice, long chat with a godly friend. You know the type of girl I'm talking about—someone who:

- Will listen carefully to all that you're saying

- Has a gift for empathizing with your crisis situation

- Won't share your private conversation with her other friends

- Isn't just listening for information's sake, but because she truly cares for you, and wants to help

- Won't allow you to wallow in sin, but will rebuke you if a sin issue is your problem

- Will give sound, biblical advice

- Will have you smiling by the time you hang up the phone, even if the problem isn't completely resolved

I wanted a friend like that all my life, and used to pray that the Lord would send me one, since he hadn't sent me a sister with whom I could share my heart in the sweetest confidence. However, it wasn't until I was about seventeen or eighteen years old that I found such a friend. This girl was worth the wait, though. Not only does she boast all of the qualities above, but she is also the type of friend who will hold your hair out of your face while you lose the contents of your stomach in a big orange bucket—I know from experience.

I can come to her tied up in knots . . . and leave talking to her reminded of the peace that only the Lord can give. It doesn't matter if I'm stressed out about a project, a nasty blog comment, or another relationship. She will *always* listen. And she will *always* remind me of the amazing God I serve.

Do You Have a Friend Like This?

We already talked in great length about how to show love to our brothers in Christ in previous chapters, but a question I don't receive quite as often is how we can show charity towards our *sisters* in Christ. Certainly, one of the ways our ministry extends past the four walls of our home is through ministering to the Bride of Christ. As we strive to minister to the body of believers, our sisters in Christ can have a tremendous place of importance in our spiritual walk. Some Christian families do not believe that their children should have close friends outside of the family setting; while I can see the wisdom of balancing our time with our peers with time spent with those older and wiser than we are as well, I can also see a biblical precedent for strong relationships within the family of faith as well (David and Jonathan come to mind).

But What If I Don't Have Any Like-minded Friends?

I attend a family integrated church here in my hometown. Our fellowship has grown from a handful of families meeting in a living room every Sunday (back around my sixteenth birthday, in 2006) to a network of diverse and passionate believers that's growing like wildfire. Every Sunday, I am able to walk into a church and know that I am going to hear sound doctrine preached from the pulpit. During the fellowship time after church, and throughout the week, I have been able to get to know like-minded Christians of all ages. I know a lot of singles, whether they're young men or young women who attend our church as singles, or young people who attend our church with their families.

I haven't always been blessed to be in such firmly-rooted surroundings, however. Specifically, I didn't make one friend the whole time I lived in Oxford—save my brother, who I had lived with in the same household for years, but who, upon closer acquaintance, I realized that I didn't even know all that well. The same can definitely be said for my parents and me. When I went to my first homeschool co-op in the States, I was flabbergasted at how many homeschooled children there were there!

Though the Bible does talk about friendships, and the importance of fellowship among like-minded Christians, I know from experience that sometimes, the Lord calls us to seasons of loneliness; and in those seasons, as we draw closer to the families he's blessed us with, he can teach us things about them, about our purpose, and about him that we never could have learned outside of the lean times. So, to answer the question, honestly, the most important element to my spiritual development was the purposeful, one-on-one discipleship of my parents; relationships with believers outside of my family is important—but secondary.

What Does Like-minded Really Mean?

Now, *like-minded* can be a broad term. For instance, on the subject of courtship: While biblical marriage and courtship are things that many families in our church hold dear, there are many different ways that we go about those courtships. There are general principles we find in Scripture (accountability, purity, purposefulness), different families and different couples, are going to execute those principles differently. As with many biblical principles, the outworkings are going to very from family-to-family. The goal is not that we all look alike, but that we are all working towards the same goal: the glorification of the Father.

I think sometimes, family integrated churches have a reputation for only attracting the already-like-minded. Of course it's important to encourage our brothers and sisters in Christ, and to be encouraged by them, but if we're about cultural reformation, we have to have a vision bigger than families who look just like us, or families that already "get it." So, no, not every family (or single) who walks through those doors on Sunday homeschools their kids, has a stay-at-home mom, or has a stay-at-home daughter. Not everyone already has children who are trained to sit still in church. Some of those other practices are an outgrowth of convictions that are subject to change and refinement. Our convictions and the practices that flow from us don't make us the perfect little church anymore than they make our homes the perfect little homes, because perfection is impossible, and that's not what we're striving for. We're about "proclaiming the supremacy of Christ with a few towards biblical conversion and discipleship..." and all that this entails. Having this common goal is what makes us "like-minded." We do not walk in lockstep, by any means, but we are walking in the same direction: We have the same priorities.

But I Don't Have Anything in Common with the Girls at Church!

Paul speaks about the attitude we are to have towards the brethren:

> So if there is any encouragement in Christ, any comfort from love, any participation in the Spirit, any affection and sympathy, complete my joy by being of the same mind, having the same love, being in full accord and of one mind. Do nothing from rivalry or conceit, but in humility count others more significant than yourselves. Let each of you look not only to his own interests, but also to the interests of others. Have this mind among yourselves, which is yours in Christ Jesus, who, though he was in the form of God, did not count equality with God a thing to be grasped, but made himself nothing, taking the form of a servant, being born in the likeness of men. And being found in human form, he humbled himself by becoming obedient to the point of death, even death on a cross. Therefore God has highly exalted him and bestowed on him the name that is above every name, so that at the name of Jesus every knee should bow, in heaven and on earth and under the earth, and every tongue confess that Jesus Christ is Lord, to the glory of God the Father. —Philippians 3:1-10

This sort of attitude leaves very little room for the "they aren't like me!" line of argument. If the girls are your church are "too worldly," seek to encourage them in Christ—if they are "too sheltered," seek to encourage them in the Lord—if you have no other interest in common, your commonality in Christ should be enough to spur you to minister to them with edifying conversation, and by demonstrating kindness and attentiveness to them, and by praying for them.

How Can We Find Friends like the One You Mentioned?

I am so blessed by the handful of close friendships I have been able to develop with mature, godly young women; however, I have found that the best way to attract the sort of friends who will edify you is to *become* that kind of friend. In my case, it was nurturing godly friendships that made me realize something: one of the reasons I had had so much trouble finding godly friends before was because I had been concentrating so much on finding someone to meet *my* needs that I had never once considered trying to become the kind of friend I was so anxious to have.

How about you? Can your friends trust you to truly listen to them when they're sharing their hearts with you—to give them godly counsel when they are seeking advice—to confront them when you know they are in sin—to love the good about them, and to pray for them when there is a need for growth? Or do you tend to only half-listen to your friends when they talk, waiting for your chance to speak—instead of giving godly advice, do you counsel them foolishly—instead of rebuking them in their sin, do you wallow in it right alongside them—instead of praying for them, do you complain about the little pet peeves you have?

Learning to Communicate

One of the main problems that we young ladies have when it comes to encouraging our friends is learning the art of communication.

When my brother Elijah was about three, someone bid him farewell with a familiar, playful greeting:

"See you later, alligator!"

Elijah, who had never heard the saying before, struck a very confused expression, then uttered the only reply that made sense to him at the time: "Bye . . . *pig.*"

Now, of course, had he heard the expression before, he would have replied, "After a while, crocodile." But he hadn't. He had also never heard anyone use the word "pig" in a derogatory manner, and so he simply answered one animal name with another.

The hearer took no offense. We took Elijah aside and explained to him what we meant by "see you later, alligator," and also, that it wasn't very polite to call people pigs.

We often laugh at that story now, and I love how the tale reminds me about the importance of good communication.

Ephesians 4:29-30 says:

> *Let no corrupting talk come out of your mouths, but only such*

> *as is good for building up, as fits the occasion, that it may give*
> *grace to those who hear. And do not grieve the Holy Spirit of*
> *God, by whom you were sealed for the day of redemption.*

So our talk should be that which is "good for building up, as fits the occasion, that it may give grace to those who hear." I think if we young women kept those standards in our minds, the world would be a much more pleasant—and quieter—place, wouldn't it? Sometimes, we jaw on idly, other times, we criticize harshly, still other times, we don't speak edifying words when we ought.

I think one of our main problems with communication is that we don't talk to edify and encourage others; we talk to please ourselves. We talk to entertain ourselves, to make ourselves look good in front of others, we talk simply for the sake of talking! But so few times are we actually speaking for the purpose of edifying and building up other believers.

This does not mean that we will never have to correct or redirect other sisters in Christ, especially those younger and less experienced than we; it does, however, mean that, even when we are confronting someone about their sin, or speaking unpopular truths, that we do so in love, in order to *build up* others, not to entertain ourselves.

My favorite definition of conversation comes (not surprisingly) from Webster's 1828 dictionary:

> *Intercourse; interchange of knowledge; correspondence; good*
> *understanding between men.*[30]

Good understanding.

That's definitely key to listening. A good way to develop a good understanding when listening to others is to actually *listen* to them!

Many times, I believe (and this because I have done it myself) that, instead of listening in a conversation, we are letting our minds wander off, we are waiting for an opportunity to change the tide of a "boring" conversation, we are waiting for our next opportunity to talk. That's not listening. To listen is to love the communicator enough to actually strive to *hear* what they are saying, to process it, to respond to it in a way that will build them up.

We also need to strive not to let preconceived notions or judgments cloud or understanding of what the communicator is saying.

When I was about thirteen, I went through this horrible emotional stage (yes, I am still quite emotional, but at thirteen, it was even worse). All anyone had to do was look at me the wrong way, and I felt like they didn't *like* me. So many times, the tone of someone's voice, a certain word they used, a look on their face would make me cry. Obviously, they were laughing at me, obviously, I was annoying them, *obviously*, they hated me!

Now, that was very foolish of me, but, at the time, I felt completely justified in my indignation. Thankfully, I have matured a little bit, and have slowly let go of the angst-ridden notion that the entire world is out to get me, but, still, I have those days where I am prone to take insult to what someone says, just because of my mood or a dislike of the subject matter or an assumption about the speaker or . . . you name it!

But if we are to develop good communication skills, we have to learn how to stop and listen—truly listen! We have to learn to stop and think when we feel our emotions rising; we have to learn to give the speaker the benefit of the doubt, and to bite our tongues until we have our emotions under control. And we have to learn how to be honest with ourselves when, after self-examination, we realize that we have been vindictive and overly-emotional; we must stop and seek forgiveness before things escalate (James 1:19-20)!

And then, there are those times when the speaker truly is being combative and unkind, when we have to respond to someone who really is "out to get us." Blessedly, the Bible is not silent on that subject. "A soft answer turns away wrath, but a harsh word stirs up anger" (Proverbs 15:1).

Even when someone is being downright *wrathful*, we must learn how to be gracious in turn. Despite our gut reaction to hatred, discord, jealousy, fits of rage, selfish ambition, dissensions, and factions, we must learn to react with love, joy, peace, patience, kindness, goodness, faithfulness, gentleness, and self control (Galatians 5:16-26).

Steering Clear of Gossip

One of the lessons that a Titus 2 woman is to teach her young charges is to avoid gossip (Titus 2:3-5)—it is a sin that many women are prone to, I believe because of our nature as relational beings. But God's Word warns against the deadly power of the tongue:

> *Death and life are in the power of the tongue, and those who love it will eat its fruits.* —*Proverbs 18:21*

Hi. My name is Jasmine Baucham. And one time, I gossiped.

And—boy!—did it come back to haunt me! Have you ever heard that saying, "If the dog will carry a bone to you, he'll carry it off to someone else?" In laymen's (non-southern) terms, the saying simply states, "If someone will gossip with you, they'll gossip about you." I wagged my tongue "in strictest confidence" and ended up getting burned—and when it all came down to it, the only person I could blame was myself.

I felt like those silly ladies on *The Music Man*. Have you seen that one?

Pick a little talk a little, pick a little, talk a little, cheep cheep cheep, talk a lot, pick a little more . . .

For anyone who hasn't seen the movie (and it's been a while for me, so the details may be a little hazy), the song centers around a handful of gossiping ladies who, as the music progresses, begin to behave more like pecking hens than respectable women. I think it's a very mild characterization of a timeless principle found again and again in the Bible:

> *Look at the ships also: though they are so large and are driven by strong winds, they are guided by a very small rudder wherever the will of the pilot directs. So also the tongue is a small member, yet it boasts of great things. How great a forest is set ablaze by such a small fire! And the tongue is a fire, a world of unrighteousness. The tongue is set among our members, staining the whole body, setting on fire the entire course of life, and set on fire by hell. For every kind of beast and bird, of reptile and sea creature, can be tamed and has been tamed by mankind, but no human being can tame the tongue. It is a restless evil, full of deadly poison. With it we bless our Lord and Father, and with it we curse people who are made in the likeness of God. From the same mouth come blessing and cursing. My brothers, these things ought not to be so. Does a spring pour forth from the same opening both fresh and salt water? Can a fig tree, my brothers, bear olives, or a grapevine produce figs? Neither can a salt pond yield fresh water. —James 3:4-12*

Webster's 1828 dictionary defines gossip as:

> *To run about and tattle; to tell idle tales.*[31]

And defines gossiping as:

> *Prating; chatting; running from place to place and tattling.*

Even with clear-cut definitions like these, many Christian young women still fall into the sin of gossip. We are hungry to have information for information's sake—we probe new visitors at our church deeply for questions, just so we can share what we've learned with everyone else—we milk a new young woman who is courting just so we can be the first to tell everyone how she and her beau met—when someone confides in us, even if we don't reveal the confidence, we can't wait to let everyone know that we've been told something intimate by a friend. And so on.

Even though I don't happen to know many young women who I would categorize as *malicious* gossips, we still need to be careful to examine why, exactly, the affairs of others are of such great concern to us. Do we wish to know more about a sister in Christ so that we can pray for her and minister to us better? Or do we just like to be the first to know new things?

As for malicious gossip, the wisdom of Arthur Pink in the article, *Evil Speaking* (1935) is an apt reminder:

> *"Do not speak evil against each other, brethren." —James 4:11*

> *That which is here forbidden, is the saying of anything, be it true or false, to the harm of another. God requires that our words should be governed by "the law of kindness" (Proverbs 31:26), and anything which would hurt or injure the reputation of another, is to be rigidly shunned. Whenever I cannot speak well of my brother or sister, I must say nothing at all. To speak evil of others, proceeds from ill will or malice— desiring that they should be made odious in the esteem of others.*

> *It is devilish to take delight in exposing the faults of fellow-Christians, and stirring up prejudice and bitter feelings against them (Rev. 12:10). God requires that our words should agree with love—as well as with truth. Since Christians are brethren, the last thing they should be guilty of is defaming one another!*

> *Except where the glory of God plainly requires it, and the good of that person demands it—we must refrain from all evil speaking of others. If we are duly occupied with and humbled over our own many faults—we shall have neither time nor inclination to dwell upon or publish those of others! If we properly heed the exhortation of Philippians 4:8, we shall cultivate the habit of admiring the graces in our brethren—instead of being like filthy flies, settling on their sores!*

> *Well may we pray, "Set a guard over my mouth, O Lord! Keep watch over the door of my lips!" (Psalm 141:3)*[32]

Amen! May we all seek the best for our sisters in Christ (1 Corinthians 13:1-13)

Battling Jealousy

The final point I want to make about relating with our sisters in Christ is guarding ourselves against envy (Romans 13:13). So many of us, although we may not struggle with the level of jealousy that Cain harbored in his heart towards Abel, but we still possess a root of covetousness towards our certain sisters in Christ.

Anyone who's spent any time at church or around church folks knows the Tenth Commandment, which is (in layman's terms): thou shalt not covet. It's pretty straightforward, isn't it? Jealousy and envy are bad things, a concept reiterated over and over again in the New Testament (1 Corinthians 3:3, 2 Corinthians 12:20, Galatians 5:20, James 3:16). In fact, one of the benchmarks of true, Christian love is a *lack* of jealousy (1 Corinthians 13:4). The green-eyed monster is a most unattractive and unwelcome guest in a Christian's life, sowing discord and discontentment wherever it is allowed to fester. But a lot of us would hate to admit that this green-eyed monster resides in our very own hearts, even today, even right now as they read these sentences.

Maybe we "mature" Christians are too "holy" to show the usual signs of jealousy. For instance, we may not envy Susy's blond hair or Anne's cute outfit or Mary's striking features.... at least, not aloud. But perhaps we envy Susy's cheerful heart, Anne's visionary father, or Mary's courtship news?

Usually, this type of feeling isn't labeled as "envy" in conservative Christian circles. It's called "admiration" or "inspiration..." we might even teasingly declare, "Oh, I'm so jealous!" Or, worse than envy, we may begin to idolize that person, holding her up as the standard for all Christian young women to follow, pining that we can't be *just like their family*, and mimicking that young lady instead of striving to be more like Christ. It is much easier to follow flesh-and-blood fantasy heroines than to search the Scriptures for ourselves, isn't it? But even though this jealousy isn't malicious in intent, we're still shrugging our shoulders at God's all-wise provision for *our* walk and *our* life and pining over someone else's place in God's plan.

Some of us may not so easily fall into the aforementioned trap, however, because we tend to be more prideful then others. Maybe we don't jump on the bandwagon and join the fan club of the most popular, visionary family around.

Maybe we—instead—criticize them, pointing out whatever blind spots we can find, or shrugging our shoulders in a superior air, "Well, Mary's family might want to do courtship *that way*, but *my family* doesn't do that, because we see *these* pitfalls in that practice." This sort of prideful criticism, I've learned (from personal experience, I'm afraid), believe it or not, can also stem from jealousy.

Jealousy is a sneaky sin, something that isn't necessarily seen as a bad thing in our culture anymore, and something that often escapes our notice when we're searching our hearts. It's something that, when conscious of, I realize that I myself fall into when faced with the opportunity. But it's certainly hard to "rejoice with those who rejoice" (Romans 12:15), when that "little green-eyed monster" is causing us to stumble.

I have learned that it can be very healthy to seek out people with attributes that you admire and to ask their advice, to let them know how blessed they are! But to set them up on a pedestal of perfection is just asking for jealousy to seep in! It's nice to see a godly family and to pray for them, but it's another thing to look at your own family as sup-par, and to become annoyed with your station in life because you aren't where another family is. It's one thing to strive to grow in Christ, and to praise Him when you see people who have grown, and realize the evidence of His handiwork; it is a completely different matter to pine over their status, to wring our hands in melancholy sorrow, or to criticize and belittle them because of their blessings.

Jealousy is easy to spot when we're being honest with ourselves, and it's even easier for others to spot when there is accountability present. It's a serious, hindering sin leading to all sorts of mischief, from discontentment, to unkindness if we don't nip it in the bud! The children of God should never be characterized by such pettiness, and it is one of the silent killers of sisterly love among Christian young women.

There is no reason for us to be in contest with one another—if there is something godly that you admire about a sister in Christ, learn from her instead of trying to find a chink in her armor; if her family has different opportunities to minister than yours does, thank the Lord for your family and search for different, innovative ways to bless others in your particular setting— maybe even try to bless the family you might be tempted to envy! If a young woman is courting before you are, rejoice with her, and thank the Lord for his perfect timing in your life (Romans 12:15).

A lot of the things I have written in this chapter are lessons that I learned the hard way. I would tell you all of the scrapes I've gotten myself into by wagging my tongue, all of my anecdotes about holy envy, and debrief you on every session I've had with my mother on the important topic of friendship. But for the sake of brevity, I will say simply this: Learning to be a good friend and a faithful sister in Christ is one of the most important lessons we as young women will encounter in this lifetime, and it is a skill well worth devoting our time to.

I still have a lot to learn, but these are just a few of the lessons I have been taught over the years. It is so important to cherish the relationships we have with our sisters in the Lord.

CHAPTER TWENTY

Becoming a Ballistic Missile

Psalm 127 says:

> *Unless the Lord builds the house, those who build it labor in vain. Unless the Lord watches over the city the watchman stays awake in vain. It is in vain that you rise up early and go late to rest, eating the bread of anxiousness and toil; for he gives to his beloved sleep.*

> *Behold, children are a heritage from the Lord, and the fruit of the womb a reward. Like arrows in the hand of a warrior are the children of one's youth. Blessed is the man who fills his quiver with them! He shall not be put to shame when he speaks to his enemies in the gate.*

Although the passage is usually used to spur discussions about family planning (and although the principle that children are a blessing is something that we should consider when making family planning decisions), it is so rich with other truths for us to consider as well: "*Unless the Lord builds the house, those who build it labor in vain. . . .*" Our ideas of success should be shaped and defined by God's Word. *Unless the Lord watches over the city the watchman stays awake in vain.* God is sovereign in all things. *It is vain for you to rise up early and go to late to rest, eating the bread of anxiousness,* because, as it's been established in this text, God is in control. *For he gives to his beloved sleep.* Because of him, we have peace.

Then the text goes on to say, *behold children are a blessing from the Lord, and the fruit of the womb a reward—like arrows in the hand of a warrior are the children of one's youth.*

My dad has always called the Baucham kids intercontinental ballistic missiles for the Lord—an *arrow* was the deadliest of weapons in King David's time—these days, a potent ballistic missile ought to do the trick.

When one grasps a vision for what an amazing hub of ministry the home can be—when we understand what a powerhouse of discipleship the family can be—the picture of being trained and sharpened for battle takes on a whole new meaning.

However, taking the arrow analogy—or intercontinental ballistic missile analogy, if you prefer—to its logical extent, doesn't it follow that daughters should be *launched*? How does sitting at home doing nothing have an impact on the outside world?

First, we have to realize that the Bible not only gives us the command to minister to unbelievers—it gives us *parameters* for that ministry. While I have had experience with those who would try to guilt me into enrolling in my local college because of the opportunity for ministry that a secular campus provides, I understand that the college campus is neither the only nor the best place for ministry to take place. If it were, the Apostle Paul would have spent less time encouraging Christians to devote themselves to building solid family units and doctrinally sound churches and more time encouraging them to go out and be educated among the Romans.

This is not to say that a Christian young woman has *never* had a fruitful ministry on a college campus, but rather to say that staying home after graduation is a far cry from giving up an opportunity to make a meaningful impact for Christ, and it holds far more of an opportunity for ministry than "doing nothing."

I cannot tell you that every stay-at-home daughter is living a productive life, serving her family and her community to the fullest, applying her mind and pursuing her passions in the context of a strong, supportive family unit. But what I *am* saying is that, while at home, she has every opportunity to do so.

I can think of the testimonies of countless young women I know. For instance, there is the girl who volunteers several times a week at her local crisis pregnancy center, and has developed a strong relationship with many of the young women there. Do you long to have this type of ministry to others? Yes, you can pursue a counseling degree from your home. Or you could do what I'm doing in the meantime and raid your family library for the six-foot stack of books on Christian counseling. Or you could get in touch with the crisis pregnancy center in town and see what days you can volunteer.

I know a family of sisters who spends their days ministering to older people in their neighborhood. They happen to be situated very close to the elderly, and spend their days going from house to house, just spending time ministering to their neighbors. Do you long to have this type of ministry to others? Walk outside your front door—cook a meal for some new neighbors and bring it over—invite them to your home.

I know a young lady who spent six weeks with her aunt and uncle out of state, working as a nanny for them. She was able to minister to their family while Mom and Dad were working every day, as well as to get some valuable practice in training and discipling younger children. I went to spend a week with her on the tail end of her journey, and saw first-hand what an impact her servant's heart had on them. Do you know a lady in church who could use help one or two days a week? How about a neighbor who could use a regular babysitter? I have another friend who is able to serve a neighbor in this way every day of the week during the time between Dad has to go to work and his son is not quite ready to go to school.

Are you passionate about music? Do you sing or play an instrument? Have you ever thought about continuing your musical education at home? I know many young women who have received their bachelor's degrees as stay-at-home daughters. I also know young ladies without musical degrees who have excelled as teachers and concert musicians, and are able to make money from events and lessons. I know one very successful harpist who has played in orchestras and won competitions and scholarships across her state—all while living at home with her family.

Do you *love* to write? Although there is an influx of stay-at-home daughter bloggers—and since I am one, I can't really knock the practice—the Internet can be a dangerous place to share your life. There are people out there who want nothing more than to scour your every post for any hint that you are being chained in your basement and forced to write nice, pretty things that will convince the outside world otherwise (okay, okay . . . maybe that's a *little* overboard). Before you decide to enter the exciting and titillating world of blogging, why don't you apply your skill to writing for the encouragement of people that you do know? I know young ladies who write annual magazines for young ladies in their fellowship, and encourage others to contribute for the encouragement and edification of one another.

One of the most popular reasons given for staying at home is learning how to be a godly wife and mother. Have you surrounded yourself with godly older women who inspire and encourage you as you strive to become a woman of God? Are you investing your time in the practices that would bear fruit as a wife and mother, or are you frittering your time away, waiting for prince charming to come along? Are you fostering the attributes of a Proverbs 31 woman in your youth? Andreas Kostenberger lays them out in *God, Marriage, and Family:*

- Is a major asset to her husband (vv. 10,11);

- Is a trusted companion (v. 11);

- Is for and not against her husband; she has his well-being and best interest at heart (v. 12);

- Is industrious and hardworking (vv. 13,27);

- Procures and prepares food for her entire household (vv. 14, 15);

- Rises early (v. 15);

- Locates and purchases real estate (v. 16);

- Reinvests extra earnings from her home business (v. 16);

- Is vigorous and energetic (vv. 17, 25);

- Produces clothes for her family and as merchandise (vv. 13, 18, 18, 21-22, 24);

- Is kind to the poor, reaches out in mercy to the needy (v. 20);

- Ensures that she and her children are properly and finely dressed (vv. 21-22)

- Contributes to others' respect for her husband and oversees her household so he can devote himself to a role of leadership in the community (vv. 23, 27);

- Is ready for the future and prepares for eventualities (vv. 21, 25);

- Displays wisdom in speech, and in the teaching of kindness (v. 26);

- Is praised by her children and husband (vv. 28-29, 31);

- Is God-fearing rather than relying on her physical beauty (v. 30)[33]

This can seem like a daunting list, and would be especially daunting if we did not grasp a vision for becoming this kind of woman right now, in singleness. What better use of our God-given talents than to bless and inspire those in the sphere where the Lord has already placed us: our homes?

That's all fine and good, you may think: A young woman can stay home for a season and prepare for the vocation of a God-honoring wife and mother—but what if she *never* gets married? Didn't she just waste her life getting preparing for a dream that is never realized?

It depends how you look at stay-at-home daughterhood. If you look at it as a cookie cutter mold wherein all of us don aprons and stilettos to march around our homes like June Cleaver look-alikes, yes . . . young women with aspirations outside of homemaking in its basic sense are going to get shot down in the crossfire, stifled and glossed over in our quest that every young woman walk in lockstep.

If, however, you are looking at stay-at-home daughterhood simply as a different *context* for using the gifts, talents, abilities, and passions that the Lord has already given you, not stifling or casting them aside, but reevaluating the way that we are using them and finding creative ways to employ them using the home as a springboard, then you can begin to thrive.

We really haven't *lost* anything. In fact, we have gained something: not only do we have an outlet for using the gifts the Lord has given us—we have an anchor in the form of the Christian family unit.

I have a few warnings to offer you as you think about coming home:

I get so many e-mails from young ladies who say that they have spent their whole lives in pursuit of the cultural ideal (college, then career), only to realize that they now desire something completely different. They want a godly husband who will lead them in the ways of the Lord—and they want children who they can raise in the nurture and admonition of the Lord—they want to be wholly committed to their families, forsaking every other dream for the beautiful calling.

And I say a hearty, *Amen!* followed by a very sincere, *Be careful.*

When I first decided to come home, I assumed a lot of things about what the future would hold for me. I assumed that to embrace a homeward calling would mean that I needed to give up every intellectual pursuit in my life and supplant it with a homemaking skill—I assumed that embracing a homeward calling would mean that my conversation could only be glorifying to the Lord if I was talking about one of those aforementioned homemaking skills—I assumed that biblical femininity was a certain list of rules and regulations that would completely change my personality.

Remember that girl from the beginning of this book? The one who wanted nothing more than to be a writer when she grew up?

I never liked playing with dolls, never cared for tea parties, and when we played dress-up, I was always the hip journalist living in her New York loft while my cousins had husbands and children. They had on frilly aprons—I had on blue jeans and a mission.

I lost a little of the melodrama (mind you, only a little) between eight and sixteen. I read authors like Harper Lee and Mildred D. Taylor, and my voice and passion as a writer was impacted by their indelible fingerprints: I wanted to write. I was *hungry* to write. And I was hungry to read great writing. John Steinbeck, Jane Austen, Ray Bradbury, Emily and Charlotte Bronte, George Orwell, William Shakespeare, Wordsworth, Yeats, Browning, and Longfellow.

I wanted to be swallowed into the world of literature.

And then there was film. Bright, bold, and exciting—such a delicate art-form that packed such a powerful punch. I wanted to be Steven Spielberg with an afro—the female M. Night Shyamalan—the Christian Peter Jackson (I know: "Peter Jackson? Really, Jasmine?" I thought *King Kong* was brilliant at the time).

I found out later that I also have this passion for art history and humanities. I love philosophy. I love ethical conundrums. I love trying to wrap my mind around Locke, Hume, Descartes, Goethe, Smith, Darwin, Bacon, Augustine, Rousseau, and so many others...

And I love drama! I love Tennessee Williams. I love to read it and I love to act it out.

And then something really amazing happened; the Lord changed my heart regarding marriage—regarding home life—regarding domesticity...

And I went from being the chick who daydreamed about growing old in a basement full of books with her brilliant novels to hand down to posterity to wanting to be a woman who passed a Christ-exalting legacy down to her children. I went from craving renowned—be it from a Pulitzer Prize or an Oscar or an Oprah appearance (okay, so I dreamed big)-to craving to please the Lord through delighting in his design for the home (which turned out to be an even *bigger* dream). I went from saying I would never in a million years settle down one day to praying for my future husband almost every day.

Let me tell you: It was a paradigm shift.

And I entered a total and complete crisis.

I mean, think about it. I'm this girl who has devoted all of her spare time to trying to be the smartest, most widely-read, most extensively well-written, most articulate female that there is (an impossible goal, I know, but I was working on it) who now wants nothing more than to be a wife and mother.

I'm going to be honest with you: At that point in my life, I was so anxious to shape myself into that ideal woman that I would have had a book burning and filled my shelves with cookbooks if that's what it took.

I went to my dad with tears in my eyes, thinking about *To Kill a Mockingbird* and how I would never read it again if it wasn't feminine enough for me to peruse, and I said, "What do I need to do in order to contribute to this household, Dad? Who do I need to be in order to become the woman God wants me to be?"

My dad didn't give a second thought to it. "I could really use a research assistant."

I had already been doing some work for Daddy, so I was taken aback. Surely when he said "research assistant" he meant "tea-service consultant" or "doily crocheter."

But, no. Research assistant it was. My dad explained that he needed me to use the gifts the Lord had already given me in order to help him. And my mom explained that by walking alongside her, day in and day out, and by hearkening to her word and example, I would be getting hands-on preparation in managing a home—unless I wanted to, I didn't have to learn the etiquette for high tea in order to be a woman of God.

I was so relieved, dear reader—you can't imagine how *completely* relieved I was!

It took my parents to show me that the best way I could help *my* home was the use the gifts the Lord had given me by becoming a research assistant, an online store coordinator, and taking over my dad's booking. It took them both to show me that the most God-glorifying conversations were still the ones that centered on his redemptive purpose in our lives—and while talking about the newest apron pattern was all right, it paled in comparison to talking about all that the Lord was doing in my life. It took my parents to show me that God created me the way I am and put me in my family for a host of reasons that I am still learning every day.

All that to say, I am not fussing at you with these warnings: I've been there and done that on a number of them—seen other daughters fall into the same trap—and am trying to save you the frustration.

Be Careful to Run from the Stereotype We've Talked About

"All the really popular daughters do this, so this is what I need to learn to love, too" vs. "This is where my gifts and passions lie—how can I use them within the context of my home to bless my families and others?" Yes, there is an element of stretching ourselves to learn those things which would help our homes run smoothly, even if we are not necessarily inclined to them (for me, it was cooking; when I first stepped into the kitchen, I was a basket case); however, there are also those things which is does us little good to yearn after (Suzie is an accomplished harpist who has played for ten years—yes, that will bless her family, but you're twenty-one, and can't take harp lessons;... what are *you* good at?)

Psalm 139 tells us that we are fearfully and wonderfully made—what things has the Lord given us so that we can use for his purposes?

Be Careful to Develop Practical Skills

There is nothing wrong with learning how to knit pretty scarves; I did it myself one summer. However, learning how to knit a scarf, crochet a doily, or serve tea, English country style, should not overtake learning how to balance a checkbook. Teach a child to read. Dedicate your time to your own studies. Serve other women in the church. Help your mother with the practical, day to day responsibilities. Aid your father when you are able. One of my favorite verses has become Nehemiah 3:12: "Next to him Shallum the son of Hallohesh, ruler of half the district of Jerusalem, repaired, he and his daughters."

The verse is so easily missed tucked in with the difficult-to-pronounce names in the third chapter of what is an obscure book of the Bible to some, but I love it: Nehemiah is rallying the Israelites to build this wall—and Shallum has a mission and a vision to obey the Lord through submitting to Nehemiah's authority—and his daughters come alongside him to help him fulfill that vision.

They're out there building a wall! Serve where you are needed—even if it involves getting knee-deep in rubble!

Be Careful Not to Lose Your Joy in Christ in the Calling of "Femininity"

I put *femininity* in quotes because we tend to manufacture a stereotype of femininity that really has nothing to do with the biblical pattern of a helpmeet who is her husband's aid and counterpart. I have seen some *joyless* girls pursuing "femininity," plastering on false smiles and playing a part instead of truly loving and serving the brethren and sincerely seeking growth and heart-change in Christ. Study the Lord's Word for his standard for his women (you will not find it written that we all have to enjoy teas, that each of us has to notice the others' fashion sense, or that the only thing we can talk about is domesticity), and strive to display a genuine love for him and his people (Matthew 17:38-40), not that love which would garner the most attention. If you find yourself floundering, losing your joy in Christ... evaluate yourself: Am I doing things just to please others? Am I trying to play a part just to fit in? Or am I truly being sanctified by the Lord, conformed to *his* image, not my own fantasy? Biblical womanhood, at its core, is merely embracing Eve's purpose (Genesis 2:18): serving those around you with the gifts the Lord has given you; making a home, yes, or being willing to pull up your sleeves and build a wall like the women in Nehemiah's day. Taking joy in the raising of children, you bet... and being able to get dirty chasing them in the backyard. Beautifying, you bet, but also possessing deeper traits than mere beauty: intelligence—competence—true joy (Nehemiah 8:10)

Be Careful Not to Fall into an Effort/Rewards Notion of Biblical Womanhood

Be careful that you're not just embracing biblical womanhood for the husband. Because, if the only reason you want to embrace femininity is to find yourself in that perfect man's embrace, you will, 1) find yourself doing extra-biblical gymnastics to get the attention of the young men the Lord puts in your path (whether you're fluttering your eyelashes, using your mom to tell his mother *just how amazing* you'll be as a wife, or cultivating a relationship with his sister in case he notices you), and 2) you will find yourself battling contentment and disillusionment the longer the Lord plans for you to be single. Remember the goal here, and in every season, is to glorify God. And so whether or not he places a husband in your path, you still have a purpose beyond matrimony, and your view in all that you do should not be to "rope a man"—it should be to please the Lord.

Be Careful that You're Not Just Holding the Line

Be careful that you aren't just biding your time for a husband. Be careful that, instead of storing up your treasures in heaven, you aren't storing up your treasures in your hopechest. Devote your times to the things that will serve others in the here and now. Devote your time to becoming a well-rounded woman so that you can be a good steward of the gifts and the time that the Lord has given you. Devote yourself wholly to God. I am not saying that you shouldn't prepare for marriage—but do so within the context of keeping your eyes trained on the goal that always supersedes it: the glory of God (Psalm 37:4).

Be Careful that Your Convictions Are Your Own

I get e-mails about everything from tank tops to first kisses to alcohol consumption. I answer every e-mail this way: "I don't care what you think of me, so you shouldn't care what I think of you." And then I delete it and say it in a nicer way: Ladies, I write for your encouragement, it's true; and I love that you like reading what I have to say. But *search the Scriptures and come to your own convictions.* Don't take everything I or anyone else says at face value—and don't fall-back on my words or anyone else's to ease your conscience when the Holy Spirit convicts you. And don't double-check with me to make sure your convictions are fine. Move forward boldly and joyfully in Christ, submitting yourself to his Word and the authorities he has put in your life.

In short, sisters, welcome home. It is an exciting, challenging place to find yourself, is it not? Keep busy, will you? And embrace each new challenge with joy and vigor! Don't lose yourself in a stereotype, okay? Look to Christ and use the gifts and traits he's given you for his glory! And don't crane your neck towards the future, all right? Live full-heartedly for Christ in the here and now. Be in genuine pursuit of his will. Earnestly seek to love and serve his people.

I hope this book has inspired you to reevaluate your at-home years as a fruitful opportunity for growth and ministry. I hope it has encouraged you to reevaluate your presuppositions regarding post-high school plans for young women. If you are already a stay at home daughter, I hope this book has provided you with more encouragement to keep striving to glorify the Lord during the precious years you have under your father's roof.

When I first started writing this book, I was so nervous that I wouldn't have much to bring to the table. I thought and rethought the structure, thought and rethought the topics I would cover, and thought and rethought signing that contract in the first place. Yes, as a stay at home daughter, I am somewhat qualified to encourage on that topic—but I know so many other young women who just "have it down" much more than I do!

I was talking to my dad about this feeling one morning, sharing the chapter layout I had planned, and getting somewhat excited about digging in when he looked at his watch. "It's getting late, babe. Don't just write about it—go do it!"

He was talking about helping him get breakfast on the table.

Every time I was interrupted while writing this book—whether one of the boys rushed into my room and started tickling my feet, my mom called upstairs and asked if I wanted to run an errand with her, my dad wanted to show me a new book that came in the mail—I was reminded of the title of what I'm writing: *Joyfully at Home*. And I was reminded of why I'm writing it.

The only thing that could possibly make me qualified to write a book about living joyfully at home has much less to do with my skill or passion as a writer than it does with my passion and zeal for my home—if I spent my days buried in my bedroom like a scientist in her laboratory, parsing phrases like Marie Curie juggled test tubes, even if my prose was perfection personified, I would have failed at truly encouraging you to spend your time more wisely at home!

What makes me excited about this book was that I wrote it amid CLEP tests and dirty diapers, laundry and house-cleaning, grocery shopping and meal planning, baby sitting and church functions, family worship and family time, sisterly antics and time spent with dear friends... I did not take a break from my life—it kept going some days when this project was put on the backburner—because, you see, this book is only important insofar as it encourages you to *put it down*!

Don't just read about it—do it!

What are you waiting for?

Endnotes

1.   Meade, Starr, *Training Hearts, Teaching Minds: Family Devotions Based on the Shorter Catechism* (Phillipsburg, New Jersey: P & R Publishing Company, 2002).

2.   Ascol, Thomas K., Editor, *Truth and Grace Memory Book* (Cape Coral, FL: Founders Press), p. 34.

3.   Grudem, Wayne, *Evangelical Feminism and Biblical Truth: An Analysis of More than 100 Disputed Questions* (Sisters, Oregon: Multnomah Publishers: 2004), pp. 30-42.

4.   Lewis, C.S., *Surprised by Joy* (Orlando, Florida: Harcourt Books, 1984), pp. 207-208.

5.   Botkin, Anna Sofia & Elizabeth, *So Much More: The Remarkable Influence of Visionary Daughters on the Kingdom of God* (San Antonio, TX: The Vision Forum, 2005), p. 16.

6.   Kostenberger, Andreas J., *God, Marriage, and Family: Rebuilding the Biblical Foundation* (Wheaton, IL: Crossway Books, 2004).

7.   *Ibid.*, 95, quoting from Daniel I. Block, "Marriage and Family in Ancient Israel," in Ken M. Campbell, ed., *Marriage and Family in the Biblical World* (Downers Grove, IL: InterVarsity Press), p. 47.

8. Baucham, Voddie Jr., *What He Must Be If He Wants to Marry My Daughter* (Wheaton, IL: Crossway Books, 2009), p. 63.

9. *Ibid*, p. 65.

10. Kassian, Mary, *Girls Gone Wise in a World Gone Wild* (Chicago, IL: Moody Publishers, 2010), p. 134.

11. Baucham, Voddie Jr., *What He Must Be If He Wants to Marry My Daughter* (Wheaton, IL: Crossway Books, 2009), p. 46.

12. (http://www.oldlandmarks.com/puritan.htm#The%20Valley%20 of%20Vision)

13. Bridges, Jerry *Respectable Sins* (Colorado Springs, CO: NavPress, 2007), p. 73.

14. Bridges, p. 75.

15. Bridges, p. 71.

16. http://www.joyfullyathomeblog.com/2009/10/people-pleaser.html.

17. Kassian, Mary., *Girls Gone Wise in a World Gone Wild* (Chicago, IL: Moody Publishers, 2010), pp. 131-132.

18. http://www.1828-dictionary.com/d/search/word,independence.

19. http://www.1828-dictionary.com/d/search/word,dependence.

20. http://www.1828-dictionary.com/d/search/word,competent.

21. Baucham, Voddie Jr., *Family Driven Faith* (Wheaton, IL: Crossway Books, 2004), pp. 163-164.

22. http://www.1828-dictionary.com/d/search/word,judge.

23. http://www.voddiebaucham.org/vbm/Blog/Entries/2009/2/6_ Searching_For_An_Affordable_College_Alternative.html.

24. http://www.collegeplus.org/.

25. http://www.omf.org/omf/us/get_involved__1.

26. Baxter, Richard, *The Reformed Pastor* (Carlisle, PA: Banner of Truth, 1646, 2001), p. 100.

27. Baxter, p. 102.

28. Ennis, Patricia A., Tatlock, Lisa, *Practicing Hospitality* (Wheaton, Illinois, Crossway Books: 2007), p. 23.

29. http://www.1828-dictionary.com/d/search/word,hospitality.

30. http://www.1828-dictionary.com/d/search/word,conversation.

31. http://www.1828-dictionary.com/d/search/word,gossip.

32. http://www.gracegems.org/Pink/evil_speaking.htm.

33. Kostenberger, Andreas J., *God, Marriage, and Family: Rebuilding the Biblical Foundation* (Wheaton, IL: Crossway Books, 2004), p. 52.

Other Books from Vision Forum

The Adventure of Missionary Heroism

Be Fruitful and Multiply

Destination: Moon

The Elsie Dinsmore Series

The Family

Family Man, Family Leader

John Calvin: Man of the Millennium

Large Family Logistics

The Letters and Lessons of Teddy Roosevelt for His Sons

The Life and Campaigns of Stonewall Jackson

The Little Boy Down the Road

Missionary Patriarch

Mother

Of Plymouth Plantation

Poems for Patriarchs

The Princess Adelina

Reformation & Revival: The Story of the English Puritans

The R.M. Ballantyne Christian Adventure Library

Sergeant York and the Great War

So Much More

The Sinking of the Titanic

Ten P's in a Pod

Thoughts for Young Men

Verses of Virtue

Other Books from Voddie Baucham Ministries

What He Must Be

Family-Driven Faith